REHABILITATION

OUR STORY OF SURVIVAL

CHRIS MAUL

REHABILITATION
OUR STORY OF SURVIVAL

ISBN: 978-0-578-63642-9

Cover Design by Chris Maul

Edited by Sydney Mire

Formatted by 90 Day Legacy Builders

Photos by Chris and Jenny Maul

Cover Photo by Chris Maul

Dedication

For my wife, Jenny, who fought for her life to stay with us. I am simply a better person because of you. You saved me in more ways than you will ever be able to comprehend. And to my children, Ruby and Charlie. Besides your mother, you are the two people that I want to make proud of me. I love you all more than you will ever understand.

Table of Contents

Preface

Struggling with negative thoughts slipping back in, those negative thoughts that can cause me to go to a place from which I had fought to escape so many times before, I went to bed praying and begging for a much needed answer.

"You must write this. You must get this out!" These words awakened me from a dream just four short weeks ago. Although it was 2:37 A.M., I immediately got out of bed, made a cup of coffee, turned on my computer, and began writing.

REHABILITATION: Our Story of Survival is a personal account of tragedy, trauma, depression, sobriety, and a will to survive. I invite you to embark on a journey-- my journey, our journey. Join me as I walk you through our story of survival told through my eyes. You will experience the highs, the lows, and the rock bottoms that Jenny and I faced both individually and together through the reality of surviving a traumatic experience.

This journey begins like many these days, with a simple text message. A number that I did not know but that would turn out to be one of the most important texts that I would ever receive--a message that changed my life and the lives of everyone in our family, forever…

Saturday, February 16, 2019 -- 11:18 AM
"Please call me. It's an emergency. Jenny has been in an accident."

One

the phone call

Saturday, February 16, 2019
10:49 A.M.

Text from Jenny:
"I'm almost to my parent's house. I'll text you when we head home. You know the service isn't good out here."

It was a cool, damp, humid Saturday morning. It had not rained, but it was a typical end-of-winter day outside. The sky had that winter gray look, and the grass was beginning to have hints of green poking through. These are the colors of winter in Mississippi. If you have ever been in the Deep South during the winter, you know this look well.

I had just finished a workout at the gym and was headed outside to do a little yard work. The weather was in the low 50's, and I did not want to pass up this chance to tidy up around the house before we had to go back to work on Monday. Jenny, on the other hand, wanted to visit her parents' house about forty-five minutes away. Needless to say, when she left, we were both a little upset with each other for not wanting to do what the other wanted. This is a typical situation for any married couple, but this time was different. This time, I could tell that she really wanted me to go with her and our children, but I was being that stubborn man who had other "more important" things on his mind for the day and was not going to budge.

I kissed them goodbye and went right to work cleaning the garage, listening to music, and getting the lawnmower ready to start mowing. Winter was coming to an end. As I was pouring a delightful cocktail of bourbon and Coke, my go-to drink for yard work, I got a text from Jenny at 10:49 A.M. with a picture of the kids in the back of the car. Six-year-old Ruby was clutching her "hankey" bundled up like always. She did not go anywhere without it. Thirteen-month-old Charlie was fast asleep in the car seat positioned directly behind Jenny. I messaged her back telling her to be careful and that I love them. That was the last I heard from them until the phone calls started.

My phone rang. Because it was a number that I did not know, I let it go to voicemail. I had been getting approximately ten or more "robocalls" a day, so I hardly ever answered the phone when I did not recognize the number. The call went to voicemail and then immediately started ringing again from the same number. I contemplated answering it this time, but since this happened frequently, again I let it go to voicemail. I still did not think much about it until I got a text from the same number.

Saturday, February 16 -- 11:18 A.M.
"Please call me. It's an emergency. Jenny has been in an accident."

I called the number immediately. At the other end was a gentleman who informed me that Jenny had been in a bad accident and that she wanted him to call me to let me know what was happening. To be honest, I did not really process what he was telling me. I did not want to believe him. It was like I was in a movie. I asked the guy how he got my number and told him that I wanted to talk to Jenny. He told me that she had given him my number, that she was having trouble talking, and that he would try to put her on the phone. The next few moments were so surreal that I still have a hard time discussing them.

Jenny got on the phone, and I could hardly understand anything she was saying. Her voice sounded like a totally different person. I asked if she was ok, and she slurred enough to say, "No, no...Not this time. I'm bad. It's bad. Daddy, please come! Our babies..." The next thing I heard was Charlie and Ruby in the background screaming. These are the screams I dream about even to this day. They were the haunting terror screams of two children who were frightened, sounds that I will never forget, and screams that Jenny and I still have nightmares about. The man at the other end of the line told me that the kids were ok and that people had gotten them out of the car. He added that they were about to begin working on getting Jenny out the car. I asked him if everyone was ok. I could tell in his voice that they were not, even though he said, "The kids are fine. Jenny is in bad shape, but she is alive." He then told me that he would text me their location.

Saturday, February 16 -- 11:22 A.M.
"It's at the intersection of 35 and Granby."

I thought to myself, "Where is that? She must have gone the back way. I have no idea where that is." I drove to the end of the road in my neighborhood, looking left and then right, trying to figure out which way to turn. I had no idea which way to go. Typically, we took a right and traveled the major roads out to her parents, but could she have taken a left and gone the scenic route for some reason?

As I sat there breathing heavily and trying to compose myself, I contemplated which way to go. Then it came to me: I remembered something that Jenny had told me the night before while we were having a typical evening in the Maul household. You know the kind-- the kids running around making a lot of noise, Jenny making some kind of crazy remark that would un- doubtedly make her laugh at herself, and our family friend showing up unannounced to eat dinner and hang out for a while. For some reason, Jenny brought up that she had enabled the location setting on her phone, just in case I ever needed to find her. Looking back, it is weird to me now that she picked that mo- ment, seemingly out of the blue, to tell me about this feature. Little did I know at the time that God was pre- paring me for something greater than I could ever im- agine. Another thing I vividly remember saying to her that evening was, "You know I can't do this life without you." She replied, "I know. Now stop saying things like that." I pulled up "location" on my phone, hoping that her location would actually pop up, and it did. I pro- grammed the GPS immediately to take me to my fam- ily.

The drive seemed to go on forever. I was driving as fast as I could with my hazard signals on, waiting to get pulled over but never did. "Turn right here. Turn left here. Proceed for 36 miles..." I wondered if this drive would ever end. I had so much going on in my head: "Is she alive? Are my kids ok? How bad is this acci- dent?" I cried out, "Lord, please don't take them from me!"

I called Jenny's parents to tell them what was happening. They were out running a few errands before Jenny was to get there and were closer to her than I was. They told me that they knew where the location was and that they would head that way and let me know more when they got there. Well, time passed, and there was no phone call from her parents, which got me extremely anxious and worried. I began to get a little sick to my stomach. Again, thoughts sneaked into my mind, "Is she dead? Is Ruby dead? Is Charlie dead? Are they all dead? If nobody is calling me, it must not be good." You see, when driving to something like this, you cannot prepare yourself for what you may pull up to. I thought I was prepared, but I was in no way close to being prepared for this reality.

I eventually got to Highway 35, a long road with many rolling hills. Each time I came to the top of a hill, I hoped to see an ambulance or a cop car or something, but there was nothing to see. Finally, I approached the top of one tall hill that seemed to go on forever. As I crested it, I saw in the distance not just one ambulance or not just one cop car but a plethora of flashing lights of different colors. I knew then that I was about to pull up to something that, to say the least, was going to be horrific. Again I prayed, "Lord, I cannot do this without them, and You know that! Please don't take them away from me yet.

Two

the scene

Saturday, February 16, 2019
12:09 P.M.

As I crested the hill, still about a mile away from the scene, I saw the large number of emergency vehicles there to assist--police cars, ambulances, fire trucks, volunteer fire trucks, and an airlift helicopter that had landed in the middle of the highway. "Please God, don't let this be for them!" As I approached, I noticed that all lanes were blocked going both ways and that cars were backed up about a quarter mile from the actual spot of the wreck. I took my place at the back of the line, threw my Jeep in park, jumped out, tossed my keys down, and started running.

Running to "ground zero," I noticed the faces of every person standing outside their cars. It was as if I was running in slow motion--like being in a dream. You know, that dream where you feel as though you are running as fast as you can but not getting anywhere. That is exactly how it felt. I could "hear" what each person was thinking as I ran past them just by the looks on their faces: "Is that her husband?" "Is that their father?" "Oh my God, this poor man." "Lord, please let this man's family be ok." "Oh, no…" "Run faster, run to them."

The looks on those faces will be seared into my memory for the rest of my life. Looks of awe, questioning, sadness, wonder, and worry. These faces, these random people that I had never seen before, were to become the faces that I saw over and over in the next few weeks and months. The faces that I saw when I was alone in the darkness trying to go to sleep. The faces that kept me from being able to fall asleep. The faces that woke me up sweating in the middle of the night. The faces that I dreaded seeing every night. I saw them during the day, when I drove, when I walked alone. Always in my mind I saw them. They were like demons drawing me in, one face at a time. Drawing me into a place that I did not like to be. Drawing me into a darkness from which I could not escape. These were the faces I eventually tried to escape from, one drink at a time.

Even months later as I write this part of the book, I can

picture these faces. I am no longer afraid of them. Some of them have faded a bit, but I still see them in my dreams and in my daily life. They hit me like a crashing wave. I cannot explain why or how it happens, but it does. Sometimes I consciously have to make myself ignore them so that they do not take me back to that dark place and so that I do not pick up a drink again. It is not easy. Sometimes they win, and for a moment, I enter back into a state of depression that I cannot describe. Eventually, I tell them to leave me alone and they disappear, slowly. These depressive spells seem to become fewer and farther apart from where they once were, but I try to be more aware of what triggers them and do whatever I can to suppress them before they take over. It is not fair, but these are the cards I have been dealt. I cannot give in.

I finally reached the cars after what seemed to be a lifetime of running. I had to stop and take it all in for a moment. I could not tell what was what and did not know where to look, where to go, or what to do. I saw a law enforcement officer staring at me. I think from the look on my face, he knew exactly who I was and what I was doing there. He did not stop me from crossing the line to investigate the scene. I immediately looked at both cars that were down in the ditch on the right side of the road but could not tell which car was Jenny's. The amount of damage both cars had made them unrecognizable. I stood there for a moment processing what I saw and finally realized that the car farthest from me and pointing directly at me was Jenny's.

I am no crime scene investigator, but the marks on the ground and the damage on the car indicated that it had gone airborne and most had likely flipped multiple times. I slowly started walking toward the car, unsure if I even wanted to see the mangled metal. The driver's side door was not connected to the vehicle; I looked over to my right and noticed the door leaning against a tree. Later, I learned that emergency personnel had to use the Jaws of Life to remove the door so that they could get Jenny out of the car. I never went to examine the door, but knowing what I know now, I wish that I had. I wish I could have seen what Jenny saw. I now understand that the door was purposely propped up against that tree so that people could see only the outside of the door.

Standing down in the bottom of the ditch next to Jenny's car, I looked around and noticed that I was alone. It was eerily quiet down there. I turned to my left to look up at the top of the ditch and saw medical and law enforcement personnel moving around like a colony of ants running around a mound that had just been stepped on, but it was like they did not even see me. I could not hear anything except the sound of the helicopter blades whirling around in circles. I looked up the hill to my left and saw Jenny's dad emerge from behind an ambulance. He was walking toward me on a mission, and the look on his face told the story without saying any words. I looked at him and said, "Do not tell me that she's dead! Do not tell me that any of them are dead!"

He did not say a word. Instead, he approached me and hugged me tight. I dropped to my knees and started to shake, cry, and hyperventilate. I felt like I was about to vomit. He told me that the kids were ok and that they were in an ambulance with Jenny's mother being checked out by one of the paramedics. He then told me that Jenny was alive but not doing well. He said that one of the paramedics working on her needed to tell me everything that was going on with her. I tried to calm myself down a little. I squatted down, put my hat over my face, closed my eyes, and tried to breathe. "Breathe, Chris, in and out, one at a time. Deep breath. Calm down. You can do it. Are you ready? Ok, let's do this."

We walked to the top of the ditch and toward the ambulance where Jenny had been taken. Multiple paramedics inside the ambulance were working on her. Her dad would not let me go inside to see her. He did not want me to see her arm and had warned me that it was really bad. I grabbed her foot and told her that I was there. To this day, I do not know if she knew if I was there or not. I told her that I loved her, that I would take care of our babies, and that I would see her at the hospital. Little did I know that she was in a major fight for her life at that very moment. I felt her leg move just a bit, and to me that was reassurance that she knew that I was there.

The paramedic pulled me to the side and said that he wanted to let me know what was going on. He took a deep breath and said, "It's really bad. She has a collapsed lung, has lost a significant amount of blood, probably has a broken femur, and at this point will likely need to have her arm amputated. However, her vitals are stable so that is a good sign. We are in the process of calling Forrest General Hospital in Hattiesburg and University Medical Center in Jackson to see which hospital has a trauma team ready to go when she gets there. We will be airlifting her to that hospital as soon as we can. I'll update you as to what we decide momentarily. At this point, this is all we really know." I turned and walked away without saying a word. I had to find our children. I had just promised Jenny that I would take care of them.

I turned and saw another ambulance parked behind the one that Jenny was in. I told Jenny's dad that I needed to see the kids. He walked me over to that ambulance and opened the back door. Inside were Ruby, Charlie, and Jenny's mom. The paramedic was examining the children and, honestly, I could not tell that they had been in an accident. Ruby smiled and said, "Daddy!" She gave me a hug and asked me how Mommy was. I told her that Mommy was injured pretty badly and that we were all going to the hospital. I told her that she and Charlie were going to ride in the ambulance with Jenny's mom so that the doctors could check them out to make sure that they were ok. I hugged them both, told them I loved them, and left them to check on Jenny.

About the time I hopped out the back of their ambulance, paramedics were wheeling Jenny to the helicopter. I watched as they loaded what looked to me like her badly beaten lifeless body into the helicopter. All I could see was blood. Her shirt had been cut off, and a large bandage, possibly her shirt, was wrapped around her left arm. It looked as though the arm was packed with ice, but I could be totally wrong. Her neck was in a brace, and there were a number of tubes coming from her body. I stopped just long enough to watch them get her into the helicopter before I started running back to where I had parked my Jeep.

Hoping my keys were still on the ground next to my Jeep, I ran back to the car. There were those same faces again. This time the expressions were even more haunting. Big eyes were staring at me with wonder and so many questions I know that they wanted to ask, but nobody talked to me: They knew that I was in a hurry to get to my family. Luckily, I found my keys on the ground next to the Jeep, grabbed them, jumped into the vehicle, spun it around, and headed to Forrest General Hospital.

"Lord, please let her live!" I kept saying to myself over and over. The drive from this part of Jefferson Davis County to Forrest General Hospital in Hattiesburg is not a short distance. Even driving as fast as I could, it was going to take about an hour to reach the hospital. I reached for my phone and immediately called my mom to tell her what had happened. I asked her to spread the word to our Florida family and said that I would give them updates as soon as I could. I tried to think of a way to get the word out to other family members and friends so that they could start praying and decided to post a couple of pictures from the scene with the following caption:

Chris Maul updated his status
February 16
NEED PRAYERS RIGHT NOW!!!!
Jenny, Ruby and Charlie were in a massive accident. All alive, but Jenny is being airlifted to Forrest General Hospital. It's very bad. That's all I know. I'm on my way to the hospital. Please spread the word!!!

I am not too sure if this was the best decision simply because my phone immediately started ringing off the hook and texts immediately started flooding in. I decided that I could not answer any of the calls or messages at this time and that social media would become the best outlet for me to reach out to the masses. Little did I know at the time that there would indeed be masses of people reaching out, many whom I know and many whom I do not know.

After I sent that social media post out, I laid my phone down and started to think. Questions started creeping in. Why wasn't I in that car with them? Why did she go this way? She never goes this way! Was she texting me back? I had just sent her a text earlier. Was this my fault? What if she dies? Is she going to die? What is she going to do with only one arm? How am I going to take care of her? How am I going to take care of our children? Is she paralyzed? What else is broken? Does she have brain damage? Will she be alive by the time I get to the hospital? Who do I call? What do I do? Help, help, HELP! What am I going to do? And the list went on and on…

Fair warning for anyone who is ever in a similar situation: Try not to think about too much. Try to stay in the moment. The mind can wander to crazy places, and that is never a good thing.

"Lord, please don't let her die. I can't do this on my own…"

Three

the hospital

Saturday, February 16, 2019
1:08 P.M.

After what seemed to be a lifetime, I finally arrived at Forrest General Hospital. Whipping my car into a parking spot near where the helicopter had already landed, I ran to the emergency room. A family friend of ours saw me running up to the hospital, and I am sure he could see by the look in my eyes that I was lost--not just lost on where to enter the building, but physically, mentally, and spiritually lost at this moment in time. He guided me to the emergency room entrance, where we walked through the automatic doors and into the hustle and bustle of an extremely busy emergency room. I do not remember hearing anything, but I do remember seeing faces looking at me again. Not the faces that were at the accident scene, but new faces that, like those of the others, are burned into my mind. The faces of wonder and crisis. Different faces than before, but the same questions and concerns nonetheless. Again, I could hear them talking to me without saying a word.

I was escorted past three policemen whom I will never forget seeing. They looked at me as though they knew immediately that I was the husband and the father of the people in the horrific accident. Rather than stopping us to ask any questions, they simply pointed the way to the room where the children were being held. At the time, I did not understand why there were so many policemen there, much less the magnitude of what was going on around me. I was simply running on pure adrenaline, and my mind had gone into survival mode.

We turned left and went down a short hallway, where a door was opened for me to see Ruby, Charlie and Jenny's mom seated inside. I do not remember any words being spoken. All I remember is seeing nurses checking on our children and me hugging Ruby and Charlie. Jenny's mom was doing her best to hold back the tears, but I saw them in her eyes. I saw the worry in their eyes. Ruby's eyes, her beautiful, usually full-o-life eyes, were empty. They were scared and sad, trying to process everything. These were the eyes of an innocent child who had been through and had seen so much in such a short amount of time. In the past two hours, these beautiful little eyes had been used to write so much trauma onto her young six-year-old brain. Ruby had most likely seen and heard things that she will never be able to forget, things that I can only imagine, and things that nobody, especially a child, should ever see. This unimaginable journey had just begun for her.

One of the nurses told me that the children looked really good physically considering what they had been through. Ruby had a few scratches and burn marks that were caused from the seatbelt. Charlie had a couple of large lumps on the front of his head that had already started to turn black and blue. Miraculously, there were no open cuts on either of them. I was informed that the doctors wanted to do a CT scan on both of them to make sure that there was no internal damage. They seemed to be a little more worried about Charlie's bumps on his head, which is understandable, since he had just turned one a month before and his head was still forming. Not knowing what may have hit him as the car tumbled before coming to rest, the medical team wanted to make sure that whatever hit him did no damage to his skull or brain. The nurses took Ruby and Charlie back to be examined.

Meanwhile, a hospital social worker came in, introduced herself to me, and said that she had been assigned to help inform and guide me every step of the way throughout the remainder of the day. She said, "You try not worry about anything for the rest of the time that you are here. I will be with you every step of the way. I can talk to family and friends for you, make phone calls for you, and get you anything that you need. I will be your point of contact. I will be with you and will do anything I can to give you the information you need as it becomes available." She was simply amazing; it was like having my own personal assistant. Never getting in my way, she was always just a few steps behind me, comforting me when I needed comfort, helping me remember what the doctors were telling me when I could not remember, explaining to me in layman's terms what was being told to me, and making sure that I understood what I was signing each time I had to sign a document. And trust me, there was a lot of signing of documents that day! Looking back on it, she really only had one job: That was to make me feel as comfortable and relaxed as humanly possible in this time of crisis, and she did an amazing job!

As the children were being examined, my social worker informed me that there were many friends in the waiting room and asked if there was anything I wanted her to tell them. I replied that I wanted to be the person to inform them. She said that she would accompany me and that all I had to do was look at her if I needed her to talk at any point.

We walked into the packed waiting room. There were friends from our neighborhood, friends that I had not seen in a while, church members whom we absolutely love, Jenny's coworkers from Columbia, my coworkers, and the wonderful lady who keeps our children while we are at work. But there were those faces again, faces that would haunt me. The looks on the faces of friends looked exactly like those that I had seen hours before at the scene and again as I walked into the hospital. The difference was that these faces actually knew me and my family and had an even more solemn look to them than the other faces that I had already filed into my mind. These faces wanted to get up and hug me, comfort me, do whatever they could to erase everything that was happening at this very moment, but they could not. They temporarily became more faces whose expressions I would try to forget in the weeks to come. These supporters would become part of our story, and I am grateful for every person in the waiting room that day. They would soon become an even more important part of our lives. These are supporters you never have to repay. The faces of friends who serve you and ask nothing in return. The faces of those who will end up helping us heal from this tragedy as well as tragedies yet to come. Little did I know at the time, the faces in this room, the ones that I would dream about and try to escape for the next few weeks, would ultimately be the same faces that would help my family heal. These were the faces that would take the place of terrible memories and replace them with hope and recovery.

I told everyone that I was thankful for their presence

but that there really was not much I could tell them at this point because I had not talked to any doctors yet. All I knew was what I was told at the scene--that Jenny most likely many broken bones and would possibly lose her left arm. Besides that, I did not know anything else. I was not in there long, and I do not remember if any of them said a word to me. Again, everything this day seemed so quiet. As I think about it, I remember seeing things and speaking things, but the majority of it was like walking down a tunnel where I could see everything and hear what I was thinking and what others' faces were thinking but not actually remembering or hearing much going on around me. I really do not know how to describe it. It was my zone, my other realm that I was in, my safe place, my place to try to process everything that was happening. It was as though my body took over and guided me through the day one second at a time.

I walked out of the waiting room and headed back to see if Ruby and Charlie were finished with their CT scans. As I walked to that room, I saw what looked to be like a surgeon talking to one of the policemen. I asked our social worker if that was one of Jenny's doctors. She said yes, and we stopped to ask him if he could give us any information. He looked at the social worker and then at me and said, "Who is this?" The social worker said, "This is her husband, Chris." The doctor looked at me, shook my hand while he introduced himself, looked down at the floor, leaned his back onto the wall, took a deep breath in and out, looked back up at me, and said, "I'm not going to lie to you. It doesn't look good."

His words were extremely difficult to hear. Words that should be limited to a television show or a movie, not real life. Words that nobody should ever hear about another family member, especially one's spouse. As he listed the known injuries that Jenny had at this point, my eyes got large as I tried to take it all in. To the best of my recollection, this is what I remember hearing:

"Jenny is sedated right now. We have basically put her into a medically induced coma and have her in a CT scan right now. We are looking for any internal injuries that she may have. This is what we know so far. She has a number of lacerations on her body. Her femur is broken. There are multiple fractures in her pelvis. She has a collapsed lung. We are relatively sure that there are more broken bones, but for now we know all of the major breaks that must be fixed. We can find any smaller ones later. The main concern right now is that it looks as though we are going to have to amputate her left arm. We are waiting on the final word on that. All of the doctors who have looked at it agree that it does not look like there will be any way to save it. Our plan is to amputate the arm now because the bleeding has to stop as soon as possible. She has lost a lot of blood. We will keep her heavily sedated until we can get back in later to repair anything we can on her leg

and pelvis. Our trauma team is getting ready for surgery now. There will be three of us working on her as soon as we get the results from the CT scan. She is fighting for her life right now, and I promise you, we are doing everything we can. I will come back out and let you know more information as soon as she comes out of the CT scan unless we need to go straight to surgery. In that case, your social worker will relay the information to you."

He then rushed back through the doors that only doctors and surgical technicians were allowed to enter. I stood there in awe, trying to process the information I had been given. I did not want to have any of it wrong when I went back to tell Jenny's parents, our other family members, and all of the friends waiting for news.

I had to face everyone and let them know what was going on. Like the doctor that I had just spoken with, I leaned back onto the wall behind me, looked at the floor, told myself to gather my composure, breathed in and out a few times, looked up, and walked through the door to talk to Jenny's family. By this time her dad, brother, and sister-in-law were there. I gave them the terrible news. All of them looked at me with blank stares as I listed off the injuries one at a time, just like the doctor had done for me. There was not a dry eye in the room except mine. I recall now that I had not shed many tears up to this point. My parental instincts had kicked in. I was in a state of shock and was doing everything I could to try not to show much emotion in front of my already traumatized children. Everyone kept telling me to be strong for them and for Jenny; inside, I was mad and torn apart. More questions started to creep into my mind. This time I was slipping into a place of blame. Not blaming Jenny, not blaming the other person, but blaming myself: Was I going to lose my wife because I chose to stay home? Was this my fault? Was Jenny mad at me? Why wasn't I there?

This is the kind of stuff that goes through your mind when you are trying to "be strong" for everyone. This is what piles up on you because you are in an internal battle between your emotions and your mind and are doing your best to be the strong person who has it all together for everyone else. This is what you cannot talk about to anyone else because nobody really wants to know how poorly you are doing at this moment.

After I had informed Jenny's parents, the children came back into the room. Ruby had an IV in her arm from the CT scan and looked drained. Charlie did not make a sound the entire time we were in the hospital. His poor little face just looked at me with his sad blue eyes. The nurses and a doctor came in and told me that both of the children looked great and that there was nothing to worry about on their CT scans. They did not need to stay overnight for observations or treatment because their scans were clear. They were to be discharged and go home that evening, which was a blessing in itself. As the discharge paperwork was getting ready for me to sign, I went to the waiting room to list off, yet again, everything that we had been told about Jenny's condition.

I remember sitting in a chair in that room and know that I made some ridiculous joke because that is what I do when I am nervous. I try to make light of a situation so that I do not have to face what is happening. I looked down at my hat on my lap and started listing everything that the doctor had said to me. At this point, I had it memorized like a record spinning out a bad song. I did not want to look up. I had seen enough sad faces for the day and did not want to burn any more of them into my brain, at least not right now. This time I choked up going through the list. I think it was because the more I repeated it, the more real it became and the more I realized that this was larger than I had first expected. The social worker put her hand on my back and asked if I would like for her to explain the rest of it. I told her no, that I needed to do it.

Nobody said too much after I finished this list. I thanked them all for being there and said that they could all go home instead of sitting there waiting for more news. I said that I was going to give social media updates from here on out to keep people informed. Some of them insisted on staying, and somebody offered to say a prayer. I do not remember who it was but do remember asking them to pray for Jenny, our family, and the family of the other person involved. Although I did not know who was at fault at this point, what I did know was that there were two families involved--my family and their family--and that they also had family in another emergency room waiting area who needed our prayers. I cannot remember one thing said during that prayer; I only wanted to be far away from all of this. I wanted it to be a bad dream. I wanted to open my eyes at the end of the prayer and be back in my bed at my house with my wife and kids next to me. I opened my eyes, and I was still in that hospital emergency room waiting area. Reality was setting in...

I said my goodbyes to everyone and started to walk back into the family-only area. One of the couples from our church told me that I needed to eat. I told them that I was not hungry and that food was the last thing on my mind. They told me that I would be hungry later and that they wanted to pick up something for me. I thought about it for a moment, could not think of anything that I remotely wanted to snack on or eat any time soon, and said, "I don't know. A burger and fries, I guess." That, my friends, is exactly how out of it I had become in a short period of time. I had just said something, not to be funny, but because I did not know what else to say. I know now that they were wanting to get me a bag of food and drinks to snack on over the next few days in the hospital, but at that moment I could not think like that. At that moment, I was living minute by minute, not about the extended stay we were about to embark on. I was thinking that we would be home soon, that everything would be all right, and that Jenny's healing process would take place in the comfort of our own home. I could not have been farther from the reality of the situation.

I walked out into the hallway and knew that I needed to post something on social media for everyone to know what was happening. The hallway was the only place that seemed to be where I was left alone. I grabbed my phone and wrote this:

Chris Maul updated his status.
February 16
Jenny Maul UPDATE: Ruby looks to be ok. Charlie's head is pretty bruised up. He seems ok, but they want to do a CT scan on him to make sure that he is ok. Jenny is not good. She's in surgery now, and I do not know what they are working on. This is what I do know: She has a broken pelvis, broken hip, collapsed lung, and it looks like she is going to lose her left arm from below the elbow down. They took her straight into surgery after her CT scan without telling me anything else. All I know is that there are three trauma surgeons working on her right now. When she comes out of surgery, she will be moved to the ICU. Thanks for all the calls and texts, but this will be the best place for me to update everyone.

Yep, I said, "They rushed her straight from the CT scan into surgery." This meant that the doctors must have seen something that warranted them to go into immediate surgery without coming out to see me first. I learned this news as I was standing in the hallway posting to social media. I asked our social worker if she had heard anything about why they had gone directly into surgery. She had not but said that she would ask around to see if she could get any information. She could not find out anything except that Jenny was in surgery.

Time slipped by so slowly. I sat in the room with Jenny's family waiting for what seemed to be a lifetime. We waited and waited for someone to come in and give us news. The social worker came back in and told me that Jenny was out of that surgery but needed another procedure done, that they were going to take her to a different operating room, and that she needed to take me there so that the doctor could explain to me exactly what else needed to be done. We were stopped as we walked by the nurse's station and were told that one of the surgeons from the first operating room was on the phone there wanted to talk to me. I grabbed the phone, not knowing what to expect. Again, I am going to do my best to stay as close as possible to what the surgeon said:

"Mr. Maul, your wife is out of surgery and doing really well. I want you to know that everything inside her is ok. She did have a collapsed lung, but we fixed that. She also has a lacerated spleen that they are going to talk to you about in a few minutes. She has been through a lot in here, and we did not think that her spleen was as big of an emergency to fix as the other injuries that we had to take care of immediately. She has multiple fractures in her spine, but none of those

need surgery. Her pelvis has a few breaks in it that will heal and multiple fractures throughout. We did have to amputate her left arm. I promise you we did everything that we could to save her arm, but there was just too much damage done to it. When we opened it up, it was mainly just fragments of bone left inside the arm. There was about a two-inch section of bone that was no longer there. The muscles in the forearm were totally severed, and it was basically being held together with skin only. We saved as much of her arm as possible. We took it a few inches below her elbow. Hopefully, she will regain a lot of elbow movement. This will help when she gets fitted for a prosthesis. Her femur was also broken in half near the top of her leg. We were going to wait until tomorrow to fix that, but she was doing so well under the anesthesia that we decided to go ahead and repair that as well by hollowing out the femur, lining the bones back up, and putting a rod down the center of her femur. The rod is held in place with screws. She will always have the rod and screws; they will not need to be taken out. She will not be able to put any weight on this leg for a while, but in time she will fully recover from this. Now, I know that all of this sounds extremely bad, but I want you to know this. She is still here with you. You still have your wife, and your children still have their mother. Typically, I cannot say that after I see someone come in like this, but she has been given another chance at life. She may look a little different, but her brain activity and all of her internal organs look good considering what she has been through. You all have a lot to go through over the next few months of recovery, but she will live and you will have each other. Do not take that for granted."

I hung up the phone, turned to the social worker, and said, "She's alive and ok. Where do we need to go next?" We rushed off to where the next surgery was going to take place and waited in yet another hallway. A lady came out and had me sign a release for permission to do this next surgery. As I sat in the hallway, the door was open as the room was being prepped for Jenny's arrival. They were listening to JJ Grey, and I smiled. We love music, especially some JJ Grey. When I asked them to keep that music on during Jenny's surgery, a nurse smiled back at me and said, "No problem."

Then I heard the elevator beep and its doors open. Several people wheeled Jenny from the emergency room operating room to this room that had been set up for her. I asked if I could kiss her and tell her that I love her. They said, "Absolutely! She is still pretty out of it and will not know that you are here, but you can talk to her." Jenny's face was scratched, her eyes were shut, and she had a breathing tube shoved down her throat. She was in bad shape, but I could see her pretty face. I only had a few seconds to see her. I touched her cheek with the back of my hand and whispered into her ear, "You hang in there. You hear me? I need you. We need you. I can't do this without you. I love you so much. You keep fighting, and I'll see you soon." With that, the medical team wheeled her into the operating room for her next surgery.

The surgeon stood outside with me and explained that Jenny had a laceration on her spleen. They wanted to go in and cauterize it to see if that would stop the bleeding. They did not see the need in putting her body through a bigger surgery and removing the spleen if they did not have to. She also told me that they had found a blood clot in Jenny's leg that they were a little worried about. They needed to go in and put a stint in place to catch the blood clot if it were to release. She said that the stint basically looked like a little badminton birdie that would be placed inside Jenny's vein so that if the clot were to release, it would be caught and slowly dissolve. Both of the procedures that they were about to do, she said, were nothing to be worried about. When the procedures were finished, Jenny would be moved to a room in the ICU. At this point we would leave the emergency room waiting area and head to the third floor ICU waiting area.

The social worker and I walked back to the room that we had been in since we arrived. I updated Jenny's family and then asked the social worker to update anyone else that was left in the waiting room. This woman was like an angel to me. She had not left my side the entire time and guided me through some of the toughest hours of my life. I thanked her for everything she had done.

I left Jenny's parents for a few minutes to call my family in Florida as I had not had a free moment to call them from the hospital until now. I walked outside and dialed my mom's number. I honestly do not remember all of this conversation, and I hate that. I had been through so much by this point that I was just going through the motions. Since arriving at the hospital, I had kept up with my parents and family through a few short texts, but I literally did not have time to call them until now. Although I did not have much time to talk, I knew that my mom needed to hear my voice, and I certainly needed to hear hers. I needed to hear someone from my side of the family. For the first time since I had moved away from Florida more than twenty years ago, I truly needed my family. I needed to see a familiar face, hear a familiar voice, hug a family member of my own, and hear them tell me that everything was going to be ok because at this point I was not thinking that way. My nerves were shot, and all I could think about was how a good drink would help me calm down a little.

These are thoughts that I had been battling for the past few months now: The constant battle in my mind between drinking and not drinking. At this point, I was losing this battle rapidly. The thoughts of having "just one drink" to calm me down were starting to take over. Thank God there was nowhere to get alcohol at the hospital, or I would have crashed and burned right there. I think subconsciously that is part of the reason that I needed to talk to my mom. Yes, we butt heads sometimes, but she knows me well. She knows my struggles with alcohol, especially over the past few years. She has been through it with my father, who has lived the past thirty-seven years alcohol-free.

I know that we did not talk that day about me wanting a drink, but I am sure the topic crossed her mind. Just hearing her voice calmed me down, if only for a few minutes. I told her that I was trying to be strong for everyone and that I was doing the best that I could to keep it all together but that I really did not know just how much more I could take. We talked about the accident and the lack of information I knew about it at this point, not because nobody had told me anything about it but simply because at this moment the only thing that mattered to me was knowing that my wife was going to be ok. We could figure out the rest of it later. I ran through the list of injuries yet again and could hear the worry in her voice as we spoke. At this point, my voice got shaky every time I shared the list of Jenny's injuries. It was becoming more and more real. I was beginning to feel it all and did not like that feeling.

My mom is one of the biggest prayer warriors I know. She relates everything in life to prayer and believes that prayer can fix anything. I told her that I needed her to pick up her direct line to God's phone and make the call to Him. I needed her to start praying hard for Jenny and our little family even though I knew that she had already been doing that. Knowing her, she had been doing that since I sent out the first message to the family hours earlier. I asked her to update the family and let her know that I would do my best to keep them updated but did not know when I would be able to speak to anyone again. Things were crazy, and I was being pulled in all directions. I assured her that I was ok and that there were people around to keep me company and try to keep me calmed down. I told her that I needed to go. She said, "I love you, Chris. You are going to be ok." I said back, "I love you too, Mom."

As I got off the phone with her, I looked behind myself and paused for a moment. There, I saw the LifeLine helicopter that had brought Jenny to the hospital. This was the first time I had seen this since it was sitting in the middle of the road at the scene of the accident. I could not help but think what she had experienced during that ride to the hospital. I could not begin to imagine the amount of pain she was in during that ride. I could not imagine how afraid she was, how alone she must have felt, and how worried she was that she might die. This was the loneliest place I have ever been. Jenny is the person I turn to when I feel lonely or when I need someone to calm me down. She is the other part of this team, and I needed her now. I needed her to calm me down, to hug me, to look at me with those beautiful eyes that look straight into my soul and tell me that everything was going to be all right, but she could not. Nobody could. I was alone. For the first time in my life, I was really alone. I took this moment of solitude to update everyone through social media before

I had to make my way back inside and to the ICU waiting room.

Chris Maul updated his status
February 16
UPDATE: Ruby and Charlie have been discharged and are going home. Jenny's left arm has been amputated. There was no possible way to save it. They had to open her up to fix her femur and pelvis. They were both broken in half. She also has some fractured vertebrae but will not be paralyzed.

She is in another surgery for her spleen and a blood clot in her leg right now. The surgeon said that she looks pretty bad physically, but mentally and vitally, she will be ok. He also said that typically they don't see this good of an outcome with an impact like this. I'm lucky to still have her. I'm in the ICU waiting room now, waiting for her to come out of this surgery. I'll keep updating everyone here. Posting is the easiest place to do so for now.

Four

the ICU

Saturday, February 16, 2019
7:35 P.M.

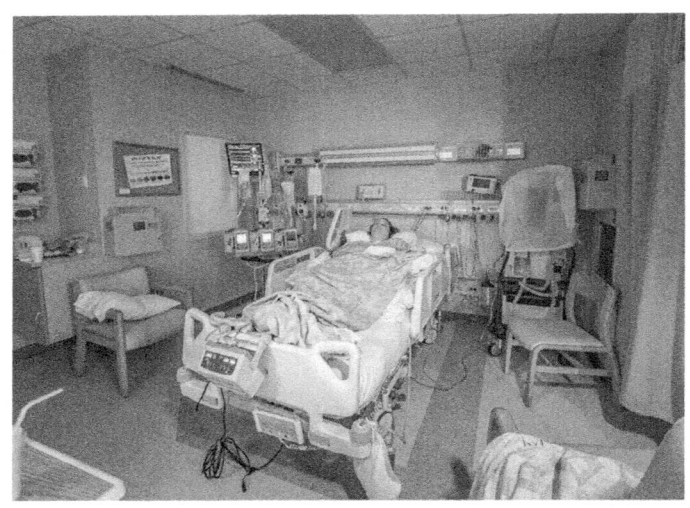

After talking with my mom, I made my way to the third floor ICU waiting room. I was dreading it because I was once told that when someone goes into the ICU, there is about a fifteen percent chance that they will not make it out. Could my Jenny become one of those fifteen percent? This is what you think about in a moment like this. When I got to the ICU waiting room and opened the door, I was immediately greeted by many familiar faces. Everyone wanted to hug me, talk to me, and know exactly what happened. At that moment, I did not want to hug, talk, or see any of them. I wanted to be alone. I wanted to get out of that building and run as far away from everyone and everything as possible. Of course, I knew that I could not do that and that having these people here would be the best thing for me to help keep my mind off everything, but in all honesty, I just wanted to be left alone.

I was told that Jenny was still in surgery and that a doctor would soon be out to talk with me. Everything was going as planned, and she was doing well. Although I have no idea why they were needed, I signed more papers. Family members and friends repeatedly asked the same questions: "What happened?" "Whose fault was it?" "What is wrong with her?" My answers were the same every time: "I am really not sure." "I don't know much yet." I again spouted "The List" seemingly a thousand times like a child learning the times tables. It almost became a challenge to see how fast I could say it and watch more faces melt into sorrow for Jenny and our family, adding to the painful collection of haunting faces I would dream about every night in the weeks and months to come.

The surgeon came out and told me that Jenny's surgery went well. Her spleen was no longer bleeding, and the blocker was in place for the blood clot. He said that he wanted to do one more minor procedure that would not take too long but would help the inevitable severe pain once she woke up, especially in her arm that had been amputated. He suggested putting in a pain blocker to help manage that issue. He explained that Jenny would most likely have pain in her left hand as though it were still there but badly damaged. Her brain would still think that she has this arm, and she would have severe "phantom pain" in her left arm for a while. The nerve blocker should help manage her pain and make her a little more comfortable. I signed another consent form, and he walked back into the operating room. I would be able to see my wife as soon as she was moved into her ICU room.

The time finally came for us to see Jenny. If you have never been a visitor to the ICU, it is an interesting place. Try to picture a large waiting room with many people sleeping in chairs, on the floors, and huddled in corners. Some are talking quietly; some are crying. The two things that every person has in common in this room are looks of sadness and wonder and knowledge that someone important to them is in a near-death situation. It is probably one of the most depressing places that I had ever been. I witnessed one family leave crying while holding a brown bag and could only imagine it contained the personal belongings of a loved one who was not going home. I did not want to leave this place the way that these people had left. I needed Jenny to recover from her injuries.

All ICU visitors had to "scrub in" at the large washing station before walking back to see their loved ones. This precaution is taken in an attempt to prevent germs from entering this area because of the nature of the patient's issues. Jenny's best friend had arrived, and we were all about to head back to see her. This would be the first time that her family and a few friends had been able to see her since the accident almost nine hours ago. Because I had seen her for approximately a minute before her spleen procedure, I somewhat knew what to expect, but no one can be fully prepared to walk into a room and see a loved one lying there the way my wife was in the ICU that evening.

As we quietly walked into the room, Jenny appeared to be resting but was still out of it. Nobody knew if she could hear us or not. The room was quiet except for the noises of monitors beeping, IV's pumping medicine and fluids into her body, and the sound of the breathing machine connected to a tube in Jenny's mouth giving her the oxygen she needed to live. She did not open her eyes right away. We just stood in awe, looking at her face. It was frightening to see her in this state. That night, we did not have much time with her.

We took turns being close to Jenny, holding her hand, talking quietly, and just looking at her. Crying when we needed to, we thanked God for her still being on this earth. I looked at her arm for the first time, wondering if she knew yet, if she remembered anything from the day's events, and what her reaction would be once she woke up and was told that she was missing most of her left arm.

As her eyes slowly opened, she looked at us, and I could see her beautiful blue eyes again. In those eyes

I saw the pain that she was going through, both physically and mentally. For the first time, I really began to cry. Someone grabbed me and told me that I did not need to do that in front of her, that I needed to be strong. This suggestion fueled the anger that was beginning to set in throughout my body.

You see, this crazy thing happens during a traumatic event: First, you go through a mode of survival, but then you slow down for a bit and start to have feelings of sadness, remorse, and anger. The anger is not anything that you mean to take out on others, but without a doubt it will come. It is natural and must be let out. I held it in as long as I could. I am sure that some could start to see it on my face at times, but for the better part of a few weeks, I held the anger in. Doing so was a mistake for someone like me. The anger came in waves, and at that moment, all I wanted was for everyone to leave me alone so that I could be with my wife. It took everything I had in me not to tell everyone to get out. I knew that being her husband, it would only take me telling someone on the medical staff that I wanted everyone out and they would be asked to leave. I held in many emotions at that moment, knowing that I was not the only person on this emotional rollercoaster. I remember saying something to the effect of, "She's my wife and if I want to cry, I can." I turned back to look at her again. This time, Jenny's eyes told me a different story.

This time I could see in Jenny's eyes that she was worried about me. We have a strong connection; we always have. Sometimes I see her and know exactly what she is thinking without her ever saying a word. This was one of those moments. I knew that she was worried about me. She knew my recent struggle with abstaining from alcohol and that if I was going to hit a wall, this situation could easily do it.

Visiting hours were almost over. Little did I know at the time that I could not stay in the room with her. The next time I or any of us would be able to see her was at six o'clock the next morning. I was not happy about this because I wanted to stay with my wife. I wanted to be there when she woke up. I wanted to be there for her and did not want to leave her side. Honestly, I was afraid to leave her side. I was afraid to be alone in our house. I was afraid to be alone in my own thoughts and worries. I grabbed her hand, kissed her forehead, and told her that I love her and would see her in the morning.

Before we left, Jenny gave us one more glimpse of hope. For both me and her friend, she did something that only we would understand--She lightly squeezed our hands three times. This is something that Jenny and I do frequently when we are around people. It is our private way of saying, "I love you" without anyone else in the room knowing.

With that encouraging signal, we left for the evening.

A good friend of mine stayed with me at the house that night, and it is probably a good thing that he did. I was not in the right mind to try to be there on my own. I got home, poured a very stout drink, and tried to sleep but could not get the happenings of the day out of my mind. There was not much sleep that night.

The next morning, I made my way to the hospital. When I got there, Jenny was already awake and looked better than she had the night before. The nurse told us that they had tried to remove her breathing tube earlier that morning and that she did well with it out. She passed the test of being able to breathe on her own for thirty minutes, but they had to put the tube back in because her carbon dioxide level was too high. She could not expel enough air to get all of the carbon dioxide out. They would try again that evening to see if she was ready to come off the tube.

Jenny's friend asked if she wanted her to read from the devotional that was kept next to Jenny's bedside at home. She shook her head yes. Her friend opened it to the date and began to read but could not continue after the first sentence. She handed it to my friend, who struggled to hold back the tears as he read:

FEBRUARY 17
My vision can be so limited. I often think that the only possible outcomes are those that I can imagine. Fortunately, my Higher Power is not restricted by such logic. In fact, some of the most wondrous events grow

out of what appear to be distress. But faith takes practice. Fears can loom large, and I can get lost in my limited thinking. When I can't see any way out and I doubt that even a Higher Power can help me, that's when I most need to pray. When I do, my actions demonstrate my willingness to be helped. And time after time, the help I need is given to me.

Today I know that even when my situation looks bleak and I can't see any way out, miracles can happen if I turn my will and my life over to God.

Today's Reminder
I have an important part to play in my relationship with my Higher Power – I have to be willing to receive help, and I have to ask for it. If I develop the habit of turning to my Higher Power for help with small, everyday matters, I'll know what to do when faced with more difficult challenges.

"In the hour of adversity, be not without hope.
For crystal rain falls from black clouds."
Persian Poem

This reading came from *Courage to Change*, the book that Jenny's friend had grabbed at the last moment before we left the house. Little did I know that Jenny had been reading devotionals from this book written for families and others whose lives have been impacted by those who abuse alcohol. This passage seemed written for the people standing in the room, especially Jenny and me.

Our time was coming to an end for the morning visit. We went out into the waiting room and came up with a plan for the ten o'clock visit. I updated everyone through social media:

Chris Maul updated his status:
February 17
6am visit update: Jenny still has the breathing tube in her mouth. They took it out for 30 minutes. She passed the breathing test by breathing on her own for 30 minutes, but they had to put the tube back in because her CO2 level was too high. She can't push it all out right now. She wanted to hear her devotion this morning. My friend opened it up and started reading...The reading couldn't have been any more perfect. I'll see her again at 10:00 A.M.

When we came back to the hospital for the ten o'clock visit, the nurses informed us that they were going to try to remove the breathing tube again while we were there. They wanted to see how she would do with people around and hoped that this would be the last time had to do this unpleasant procedure to her. Jenny did great! She passed the thirty-minute breathing test, and her carbon dioxide levels looked good. She needed to wear a small oxygen mask over her nose, but we could move her head up just a bit in the bed and she was able to drink a Diet Coke. This action may not sound impressive under normal circumstances, but considering that twenty-four hours ago Jenny was clinging on to life, this was a major improvement.

I also learned that the doctor had come in and told her about her injuries: Jenny now knew about her arm. When I saw her, she had a tear in her eye. We did not discuss it; we did not have to. I knew that she understood what was going on and that some of the reality of the situation was beginning to set in with her. She still could not talk, but I could imagine the questions and thoughts going through her mind. Her mom and friend decided to try to clean her up a little. They found a few washcloths and soap and wiped dried blood from her face. They carefully cleaned her while trying their best to comfort her in this dark time.

Again, our visitation time flew by, and before we knew it, it was time to leave until the evening visit. A nurse told us that Jenny was doing much better with family around and that if one of us would like to stay that evening when visiting hours were over, we could. Not only did I want to take care of Ruby and Charlie, who were not in the hospital, but I also wanted and needed to be with my wife as well. Jenny's mom and I had to come up with a plan--a plan in which Jenny would never be alone. From this point on, there would be times that she stayed with Jenny, times that I would stay with Jenny, and times that one of her friends would stay with her. Someone would always be close.

That evening, I was in the shower getting ready to go back to the hospital for the final visit of the day. Suddenly, the lack of sleep, the influx of emotions, and the glass of bourbon that I had just drunk collided. I got out the shower, locked the door to my bathroom, sat in my closet, and called my dad. For the first time since the accident, he and I communicated. He said, "I knew this was coming. I had not reached out to you yet because I knew you would contact me when you were ready." I explained that I was slipping into a bad place. My mind felt as if it were escaping me, and I did not know how I was going to be able to get through all of this. I felt helpless and as though I should be lying in that bed, not Jenny. Dad told me that I needed to calm down, let out my emotions for a while, stop worrying about everyone else for a moment, and take care of myself. He said that I needed to step back from everyone else for a moment and concentrate on my wife and kids. We talked for a few more minutes before hanging up. Before leaving for the hospital, I composed the last of my social media updates for a while:

Chris Maul updated his status
February 17
I write this with the sincerest of heart as I sit in my closet. THANK YOU to all of you. I have to go back and see Jenny at 6pm but I need everyone to understand that I need a break. I have one hour of sleep in me at best. I am having a hard time making decisions about everything. I talked to my father for the past 15 minutes and he gave me some advice that I will follow. I need everyone to understand that I have hit a wall. I need my space and time to be with my wife. I am so over-whelmed right now. I have my wife back. I shouldn't have her back, nobody thought she'd be back. She

told her best friend to make sure that I am ok. She didn't worry about herself, she's worried about me. She's stronger than I am and she knows it. Please, please, please contact the following people if you need any information on how to help. Please don't take offense to this. I just need my space.

The next few days were a blur. When I was at the hospital, I was doing my best not to show emotion to Jenny, listening to nurses and doctors, and trying to remember everything that we were supposed to be doing to make her recovery easier. When I was not at the hospital, I was collecting information for our insurance and our lawyer or watching the children, trying to make their lives as normal as possible. I did what I could to survive throughout the days on very little sleep. I was afraid to sleep. Every time I shut my eyes, I relived everything. I saw the many faces that I had seen over the past few days, and I answered the same questions that were repeatedly being asked. I did anything I could to sleep, but nothing worked. Many nights I lay awake thinking and writing everything down. I was running on adrenaline and suppressing my feelings as much as I could in order to survive. I am not proud of the way that I handled some things, but I was doing all I could to get myself through this. I was in survival mode, and I was losing.

After the third day in ICU, Jenny was discharged from the ICU. She had won this fight! My wife would not be one of those fifteen percent who did not make it out of the ICU.

Five

she remembers

Monday, February 18, 2019
11:37 A.M.

This chapter reveals accounts of two of the people who were at the scene of the accident. It is what they remember. (I do not know the other side of the story and do not feel it imperative to dive into it.) It details what Jenny and other witnesses remembers from that near fatal day, as well as what is written in the police report. It is the only chapter in which the names of other people are used. I feel that it is important to provide them, as I am stating firsthand accounts of heroic measures taken to save Jenny's life on that horrific day.

Jenny's Story

The second day in the ICU, Jenny got her breathing tube removed and was relieved that she could begin to talk a little. She spoke very softly because she was in so much pain. I did not want to ask her too much about anything at the time, but there were a few questions that our lawyer needed to ask her so that we could start trying to figure out insurance issues we were already facing. I told her that I knew she probably did not remember much but that I needed to know when she was ready to talk to him so that I could let him know when to come. She looked at me and said, "I remember." I said, "You remember what?" She replied, "I remember everything. I remember it all."

She began to talk, and it was difficult to listen to the details. I remember not saying much, but I listened and tried to soak it all in. She spoke slowly as she described the incident, "I was driving north on 35 when I noticed something to my left. By the time I realized what was happening, it was too late. I never had a chance to swerve or hit the brakes. I remember it all, hearing the sounds of squealing tires and seeing his face as our cars collided. He had to have been speeding. I do not think that he stopped at the stop sign. I was instantly knocked unconscious until we came to a stop. I didn't know where we were or how bad things were when I came to and began to look around." She paused for a moment before going into more details. "The pain and the sounds were unimaginable. Charlie was crying, Ruby was screaming, and I was in so much pain that I did not know what to think. I will never forget hearing their screams that told me exactly how scared my children were. I remember looking down and seeing my arm stuck in the door with bones sticking out of it. I was terrified and could not move.

"A man came quickly to try to help me as other people got Ruby and Charlie out the car. He asked me if there was someone he could call, and I gave him your number. After I spoke to you on the phone, I slipped in and out of consciousness. He tried to keep me awake. Paramedics had arrived, as well as someone who started trying to get me out of the car. I was trapped inside the car with my arm trapped in the door." This explains why the driver's door was purposely leaned up against the tree not facing the road. The amount of blood and tissue inside that door was unimaginable.

"I remember hearing people talk, telling me to stay awake and asking me questions I could not answer. Everything hurt so badly. There was blood everywhere, and I had trouble staying awake. I tried to stay calm but couldn't. I remember thinking that I was going to die and hearing the paramedics say that I was bleeding out and wasn't going to make it." Jenny then looked at me as seriously as I have ever seen her look and said something that I will never forget: "You know why I stayed awake?" I said, "Because of our children?" She replied, "No, because of you. I knew that you needed me.

"I remember the sound of rescue personnel using the Jaws of Life to get the door off so that they could get me out of the car. It was loud, and I could hear metal ripping apart. My daddy was there when I was extricated. He picked me up and carried me to the top of the hill. My leg hurt so much that I could do was scream in agony. I did not know how badly it was broken, but I knew that it was. Paramedics loaded me onto a stretcher and into the ambulance."

Jenny did not go into too much detail about what happened in the ambulance. I do know that the last thing she remembers is being loaded into the helicopter and begging for something to take away the pain. She remembers a lady telling her that they would do what they could to help her before adding, "I don't know if you are a praying person or not, but if you are, you had better start praying now." I have not asked Jenny many more questions about that day.

Wayne's Story

Wayne is a friend of Jenny's family who showed up at the scene of the accident out of pure luck that day. He is a local firefighter who has been a friend of Jenny's for the past twenty-five years. I cannot thank him enough for being on the scene; he is one of the angels who saved her life. About a week after the accident, a friend of mine told me that Wayne might have been one of the people who helped extricate Jenny. I immediately contacted him to tell him thank you. I asked if he would mind writing something I could include in this book. Within an hour, he sent me the following email:

"On the morning of February 16, 2019, my family and I were returning to Prentiss, MS from Sumrall, MS. My wife Kathryn and I and my daughter Mary Ella had been to Mary Ella's Upward basketball game at Sumrall First Baptist Church. We were at a 4-Way Stop in Bassfield when I heard Bassfield and Granby Fire Departments being dispatched to a two car '10-50' on Highway 35 at Granby Road. Almost immediately, dispatch upgraded the call to a two-car 10-50 with entrapment. Even though this was not a Prentiss Fire Department call, I made the decision to respond to the scene to assist in any way I could. I, along with one Sheriff's Department deputy, arrived on scene within five to seven minutes of the initial call for help. I proceeded to check the nearest car to me. That driver was not trapped, so I then went to the second car. Upon seeing this car, I radioed in to Prentiss Fire Department to dispatch Prentiss Fire Department's rescue truck with their Jaws of Life. I also requested additional ground unit ambulances as well as a helicopter.

"Shortly thereafter, Bassfield Fire Department and Granby Fire Department arrived on scene. We began using Bassfield's Jaws of Life to disentangle the one occupant of the car. Prentiss then arrived on scene, and we began using their Jaws as well. Jenny, who I still did not recognize, was surrounded by who I later referred to as God's angel, a black man who held her

head and spoke words of encouragement to her the entire time. To this day, I still do not know who that person was.

"This was not an easy extrication because Jenny's arm was twisted in the door and the door had to be opened. We knew when we freed her arm, we needed to get her into the waiting ambulance immediately. I give credit to BJ Wilson with the Bassfield Fire Department, as well as other volunteers from each department who were there opening the car to get Jenny out. BJ did most of the extrication. I was basically the Incident Commander on scene making sure we had all the resources we needed, as well as instructing on the best ways to get Jenny out of the car. Our on-scene resources consisted of one pumper and one rescue truck from Granby, one rescue truck with Jaws from Bassfield, one rescue truck with Jaws from Prentiss, two ambulances from AAA Ambulance, one ambulance from Covington County Hospital, and two helicopters.

"At this point, I still had not recognized Jenny. I had stepped away from the car Jenny was in to obtain an estimated time of arrival on a helicopter when I saw Mr. David, Jenny's father. Based on his facial expressions, I immediately asked him if that was Jenny in the car, and he said yes. Jenny's mom was in the ambulance with your two children and they were ok. I then went back down to the car, as they were getting the

door open. At this time, we were fully able to see Jenny's arm and comprehend the severity of her injuries. There was no doubt in my mind she would lose her arm, and my statement to my wife when we left the accident scene was without God's intervention, I was scared Jenny would die due to her injuries.

"We assisted AAA Ambulance with getting Jenny into the Rescue 8 helicopter and watched as they lifted off en route to Forrest General Hospital in Hattiesburg. I honestly thought that was the last time I would see my friend alive, but PRAISE GOD I was wrong.

"As far as what the scene looked like, looking back now, I must say it was very organized. Each department worked well with each other, and everything went as smooth as we could have hoped for. I also give credit to the AAA Ambulance crew who cared for Jenny before the helicopter arrived on scene. Jenny could not have been in better care. They were awesome in my opinion. Hats off to them and the flight crew on Rescue 8."

I have provided these details not to gain sympathy but in preparation for the next chapter. Everything to this point has been a lead up to my own personal rock bottom and my own fight for survival. The events that unfolded on this day ultimately drove me over the edge and set my life into a downward spiral that I could no longer escape on my own.

Fast forward to October 4, 2019. I was driving the family to pick up pizza so that we could go home and have a movie night. Jenny reached over with her prosthetic hand and held my hand. She stared out the passenger side window looking up to the sky and said, "You know, it is a weird feeling and place to be when you are in limbo, not knowing if you are going to die or not." I said, "I bet it was scary." She replied, "It's more than that."

Six

sobriety

Wednesday, February 27, 2019
9:30 AM

I was not going to include this chapter until yesterday, September 19, 2019, when I ran into an old friend that I had not physically seen in a few years. She and I talked about so much in a short amount of time. I told her of my plans for this book about Jenny and her accident, Jenny's recovery, and our journey throughout it. I also mentioned that I had thought about including a chapter about my sobriety but instead wanted to focus on our family. I did not want to dilute it by focusing on my struggle with and recovery from addiction. Little did I know at the time that this book would become my whole story of my rock bottom and my recovery from alcoholism. She replied that my struggle was an important part of our family's story and needed to be told. Then she added something that I have not been able to get out of my mind: "Chris, you have to tell people about your time in rehab and your alcoholism. Somewhere there is a husband and father going through this same issue who needs to hear your story."

This simple statement spoke volumes to me. So here I am at 3:00 A.M. the next day beginning a chapter that is an insight into my struggle with addiction and my battle to stay sober. Opening up about my deepest secret and being totally honest with strangers about the one thing in my life that I could not control is difficult. I am actually a little nervous and hesitant to make this struggle public; however, I strongly feel in my soul that I am supposed to do so for the person reading this right now who needs to hear it. I am going to divulge more about myself to the public than I ever have before, but I feel it necessary to do so.

This friend also told me yesterday that she was at the ICU visiting a family member the same day that Jenny was admitted and learned of Jenny's accident. She knew that she needed to help us somehow, but how? Then she added, "It's taken seven months, but the answer has surfaced, and we both know that God's timing is perfect. This was the time that He wanted you to run into me." As a result of our meeting, I feel compelled to write this part of my story.

Step 12 of Alcoholics Anonymous states the following;

"Having had a spiritual awakening as the result of these steps, we tried to carry this message to alcoholics, and to practice these principles in all our affairs."

It is time for me to put Step Twelve into action for that person currently sitting in the same spot I was seven months ago, the person holding that bottle needing to know that there is a way out. I have been to that scary place, and I know that you, too, can get through. If you do not read any other chapter, please read this one and know that you are not alone.

Full disclosure--this chapter will be long. It will begin with a few first-hand accounts of some of my experiences as an alcoholic, my experiences in rehab, my experiences after rehab, what I have done to stay sober, and a few of my thoughts about addiction and recovery. Think of it as a book inside a book.

Alcohol has been part of my life for as long as I can remember--from watching my dad fight his battle against alcohol addiction when I was only nine years old to finally realizing that I would have to wage my own battle against it at the age of forty-four. If this chapter does not appeal to you and you prefer to get back to reading about Jenny's recovery, feel free to move on to the next chapter; I will not be offended. I will never even know you did not read it! On the other hand, if you are a person who does or might have a problem with alcohol or with addiction of any kind, or if you love someone who does, this chapter is for you.

I. The Backstory

My struggle with addiction began twenty-eight years ago in 1991 at the age of sixteen. I remember it like it was yesterday. It happened after my first high school baseball game when I had my first "real" beer. Sure, I had had a few sips of alcohol before that day, but this was my first full cup of beer without adult supervision. I remember the smell, the taste, the feel of holding it, and the feeling I had after drinking it. I also remember the freedom it gave me to express myself and to open up and talk to people. Those who really know me know that I have not always been the most outgoing person, especially with people that I do not know very well. Talking to unfamiliar people can be a struggle for me, even in my adult life. I learned quickly that having a little alcohol in my system made conversation easy for me. It relaxed me, opened me up, and freed me from anxiety that imprisoned me from others.

As years passed, I learned that if I had a few drinks in me, I became the life of the party. The guy you could count on if you wanted to have a good time. The guy who was willing to try just about anything at least once, especially if I had a few drinks in me. Although I did not realize it at the time, this feeling of freedom and relaxation would ultimately be what I chased for the next twenty-eight years of my life. Over time, alcohol slowly controlled every aspect of my life, and, in the midst of it, I had no clue it was happening.

II. Do I really have a problem?

There comes a point in an alcoholic's life when he asks himself this question. I had moments like this on more than one occasion but always chalked it up to simply having a good time. I also spent my time comparing myself to everyone else I knew who drank as much as I did. Like any other alcoholic, I tried to normalize my drinking. For me this started about four years ago after flying to my best friend's 40th surprise birthday party in Orlando, Florida.

My flight was to leave New Orleans at eight o'clock that morning. Arriving two hours early makes checking in swift. Having about an hour and a half to kill before boarding, I decided to head over to the bar and start the morning with something that would calm my fear of flying. I ordered a tall beer. My plan was to have only one to help me fall asleep for the hour-long flight to Orlando. A businessman drinking a bourbon on the rocks struck up a conversation with me. He told me he had traveled worldwide because of his business and asked me where I was headed. Four rounds of bourbon on the rocks and ninety minutes of conversation later, I heard the last boarding call for my flight and sprinted to catch the plane for which I had arrived so early.

I ordered a bloody mary as soon as the flight attendant made her rounds. Finishing it, I ordered a double bourbon on the rocks, knowing that I could make it last until the plane landed in Orlando. After landing, I had just enough time to grab lunch and another beer before heading to the parking lot. My sister-in-law picked me up to head to their house in Lakeland. On the way, she complied with my request to pick up a six pack of beer so that I could have a couple brews for the ride there. I was on vacation and rationalized that it was ok to drink this much on vacation. (At this point, I had had at least eight drinks before noon!) I still had a full day of fishing in Tampa Bay with my brother, nephew, and dad and would have a few more glasses of bourbon to end the evening.

I must be transparent and tell you that I did not typically drink all day like that. I woke up the next day, went for a run, and wondered how I drank so much and could still function the next morning. Most people would have spent the next day in bed feeling like death. Not Chris--I was up at six o'clock running. I remember thinking on that particular run that I needed to slow down the drinking. I had this feeling that the amount of alcohol I was able to consume was not normal, and I wanted to change, but how?

Later that evening, my brothers and I were going to my

best friend's birthday party in Orlando. Around noon that day, I decided to have a bloody mary and a few glasses of bourbon to help my stomach feel a little better. While I had been able to run that morning, I still had a bit of a hangover from drinking all day the previous day. Many of you know that when you feel bad after a previous day of drinking, sometimes you think you need a few drinks the next day to take the edge off the hangover. Because I knew that this important evening could end up bad if I went all out drinking like I had done the night before, I decided to take it as easy as possible.

That evening, I had a blast at my friend's party. Seeing old friends from high school, many of whom were at the same party where I had that first beer, was wonderful! These were the guys I had spent so much time with in the 90's, but when I left Lakeland after graduation in 1994, I had never had the urge to return home. This was the first time I had seen this many old high school friends in the same place at the same time since leaving for college. Needless to say, there was a bit more drinking than planned. However, I kept it much more under control than I had the day before-- probably because I knew that I had to catch a flight back to New Orleans the next morning. There is absolutely nothing fun about flying with a hangover.

The next morning found me again in an airport with an hour or so to kill. This time, I went to the airport bar to have one bloody mary and catch a little of the Tampa

Bay Buccaneers football game before my flight. The bartender asked, "Would you like to make it a double for one dollar more?" It was my lucky day! "Absolutely!" I replied. I finished both drinks and felt great getting onto the plane. I ordered one double bourbon and ginger ale to sip on throughout the flight. Looking out the window of the airplane, I seriously began to question my drinking. For the first time, I thought to myself, "Do I really have a problem?"

III. My first attempt

Weeks had passed since my return from Florida, but that crazy weekend was still fresh on my mind. I was back to my daily routine: wake up, go to the gym, go for a run, go to work, come home, have a few drinks, enjoy my family, have a drink or two more, and go to bed. I rarely woke up feeling bad, and I never drank until I got home from work. I cannot say that I did not anticipate having a drink while I was at work, but I never had the urge to drink while at work. I considered this anticipation normal. After all, I thought, "Doesn't everyone who drinks do this?"

I remember going out for a long early morning run one Sunday before church. It was a normal cool fall morning, but for some reason I could not get the thought of that same question out of my mind: "Do I really have a drinking problem?" It had become a recurring thought. When I am out on my long runs, I have time to think about many things, including life, family, what I am going to do that day, and other endless topics. That day, however, all I could think about was my drinking and I remember deciding to pray about it. I asked God to let me know what I needed to do. I remember asking Him if I was drinking too much and telling Him that I was going to slow down. I made a promise to myself and to Him that I would no longer let alcohol control my thoughts, that I would slow down my drinking, and that if I was unsuccessful, I would seek help.

The following Saturday, I decided to go to a friend's house in the neighborhood for a day of smoking ribs and watching college football. This is a typical Saturday afternoon in south Mississippi--food, football, friends, family, and alcohol--and is what so many of us look forward to during the fall. The weather was absolutely perfect. A small cold front had come through, and the highs that day were in the low to mid 60's with clear blue skies. We could not have asked for a better day. I went to the store that morning to buy ribs for the smoker. By the time I got home and got them seasoned, it was time to head over to my friend's house to get the smoker going.

The games were just starting as I arrived. Like clockwork, we got the smoker started and poured a couple of bloody mary's to get our typical Saturday afternoon started. We reclined in our chairs and began to watch the game while sipping on the first of what would turn out to be way too many alcoholic beverages through-out the day. By the time people came over to eat, I had probably consumed more alcohol than a normal per-son should, but, once again, most people had no clue how much I had drank. You see, when I made my drinks, I did not pour a normal shot for myself. Instead, I poured a minimum of a shot and a half of whatever spirit I was drinking, even though the other person was having only a shot. At this point in my drinking tenure, I needed more than most people to feel the "buzz."

Jenny and Ruby were now there, as well as a number of our friends. The doors and windows were open so that we could enjoy the cool air and listen to our chil-dren playing outside as we ate inside and enjoyed more college football. At this point, I was most likely drinking beer as I typically did to make sure that the liquor would not get to me so that I could actually make it through all of the day's games without getting too drunk. After that game was over, Jenny decided that she and Ruby were going home. Looking back, had I been a normal drinker who could control the amount of alcohol ingested into my body, I would have gone home and enjoyed time with my family. The dark reality of it is that I chose not to do so. I now know that I had zero control once I took that first sip of alcohol and be-came a different person. Knowing that Jenny wanted me to come home, I said, "I'll be home in a bit." To be honest, I had all intentions of heading home.

Unfortunately, I now understand that I was absolutely

powerless to the alcohol once it entered into my system: No matter what I wanted to do, the liquor always won, and I followed whatever it told me to do. Needless to say, it happened again. I kept texting Jenny, assuring her I would be home soon, until I finally asked if it was ok for me to finish watching the rest of the late game before I came home. She always said yes; I am sure she knew that there was no use in trying to get me to come home, and, honestly, she probably did not want me to come home in this state. Given my condition, conversation and quality time would be pointless. So there I was, drunk again and needing to get home.

I had less than two miles to get home through the neighborhood. I would take it slow, just like I always did, and it would be totally fine...These are the thoughts of an alcoholic. You know the best route to get to and from places to avoid running into a police officer. You know the way home like the back of your hand. You know every turn and every obstacle that you may face along the way. Yes, I got into the car and drove home. It was about ten o'clock, and my family was asleep. I most likely stayed up and poured one more bourbon before I went to bed. "Most likely" because this was my usual pattern on nights like this.

The next morning, I felt terrible, physically and mentally this time. I could tell that Jenny was not happy with me, and I tried my best to pretend that I was not hungover. The last thing I wanted to do after coming home late was to be in a hungover state and in a bad mood. I decided to go for an early morning run while Ruby was asleep and Jenny was drinking her morning cup of coffee. I know a run sounds like the last thing you would want to do with a hangover, but it was what I needed to escape the house for a bit.

Runs were not fun when I felt like this, but they were my way of trying to give my body a jumpstart on the healing process from the night before. I remember this particular run very well, thinking that just yesterday I was doing this exact thing--running and thinking about my drinking and how I had just promised myself and God that I would either slow down or get help. Well, here I was the next day, hungover, trying to remember driving home, and telling myself that I did not need outside help yet. I just needed to make some rules for myself, and that is exactly what I did on this run: I came up with a set of rules that I was going to enforce upon myself. Rules that were going to be easy to follow. Rules were going to make me a social drinker once again. After all, at one point in my life, I had been a social drinker who did not need to drink every day of the week. Surely I could become that again.

IV. My Second Attempt, The Rules…

Rule 1 – No drinking anything with alcohol during the week. I could, however, have a non-alcoholic beer if I desired one.

Rule 2 – On weekends, I was allowed to have two to three beers each day.

That was it, two simple rules to live by. Two rules that seemed pretty fair to me. Two rules that I knew I could follow, or could I?

I learned quickly that zero drinking during the week was going to be difficult. I loved a beer or a bourbon when I came home from work and felt as though I deserved a drink as a reward for getting through a day at work. I loved everything about that evening drink. Sitting on the front porch with Jenny and Ruby with a bourbon. Cooking an evening dinner with a glass of wine. Watching television with a good beer. I can actually feel the sensation and desire for one of those moments with a drink in my hand even now as I write this. Although missing the buzz that I got from drinking, I was doing ok for a while. I made it through the first few weekends following rule 2 but realized that a couple of beers a night on the weekend did absolutely nothing for me. Unfortunately, my alcohol tolerance was so high that I eventually found ways around my rule.

I went from a few normal beers to a few higher alcohol content beers. This worked for a while. I would catch a little buzz if I drank three of them on a weekend night, but those beers are so heavy that I did not want to drink three of them. Eventually, I switched to three glasses of bourbon a night on the weekends. Now we were in business! I could drink something that I liked, and it made me feel good. The only problem with pouring your own bourbon is that nobody sees just how much is poured into the glass. Within a few weeks, I went from using a shot glass for each pour to free pouring each glass. Needless to say, these three drinks a night basically became six drinks a night, but I was ok with that. In my alcoholic mind, I was still doing better than I had been a month or so before.

As time slipped by, I started believing that I had control over the alcohol and started slowly introducing week-night drinking back into the equation. One drink every now and then during the week soon evolved into a min-imum of one drink every night. Within a few months, I was drinking as much as ever, but nobody else knew. I waited for Jenny to step out of the kitchen to pour a little more bourbon into the same glass. At the time, I did not think that I was not doing it to hide the fact that I was drinking. I just did not want to hear my wife say anything about it.

I eventually gave up on my two rules and went back to drinking the same amount as before, but this time I no-ticed something a little more disturbing to me. I inad-vertently made a point to head to friends' houses where I knew I would be offered a drink. Looking back, I realize I did this because doing so did not allow Jenny to keep up with how much I had to drink on any given evening. At this point, I had not had any crazy drunk nights, and I truly believed that I was drinking no more than most people my age. I was blinded by the fact that I was pouring a larger shot than other people and that I basically thought all the time about when I would be able to begin drinking that evening. I started doing a little research, so where did I turn for information? I Googled it!

I stumbled upon an interesting read about "high-functioning alcoholics." This term was nothing that I had ever heard until I read about it. Much of the information on topic page sucked me in, but the following passage is what I related to most:

"A high-functioning alcoholic is able to consume far more than the recommended amount of alcohol, with no visible ill effects. Such a functional alcoholic is able to raise a family, communicate with friends, and successfully maintain a career while drinking large amounts of alcohol on a regular, if not consistent basis. However, a functioning alcoholic may well be hiding symptoms of extreme alcohol abuse, such as memory lapses, known as blackouts. In addition, a high-functioning alcoholic may actually exhibit improper social behavior at times, without even realizing that he or she is acting in an untoward manner."

All of this sounded way too familiar and frightened me a bit. I refused to think that this was me but was intrigued knowing that I related so closely to this definition of an alcoholic. I spent quite a few hours looking at different posts and taking the "Do I need help?" or "Am I an alcoholic?" tests that are easily found on the internet. I even tried to trick them a few times, and surprisingly even those tests resulted in "Maybe you have a problem." I refused to admit to myself that I was an alcoholic, but the seed was planted.

V. My Third Attempt

Finally, it was here--Thanksgiving Day 2018! Thanksgiving is my second favorite day of the year, just behind Christmas Day. It is my day to make memories for our family, my day to do everything for them so that they can just sit back and enjoy the moment. If you know me, you know that this day officially opens the Christmas season and the night that the Gris-Maul Family Christmas lights are turned on for the season. It is a big day around our house! Like every other Thanksgiving Day, I woke up early, made a cup of coffee, turned on the television to watch the Macy's Thanksgiving Day Parade, and started preparing all the food for the day.

Jenny and I both love a mimosa on days like this. For her, it is a relaxing tradition that we do together each Thanksgiving. For me, it was the same, but it was also a reason to start drinking early and keep that high going all day. If I started slowly and drank at a slow pace, I could go all day without anyone having a clue how much I had drunk. I did just that, sipping on every type of alcohol we had in the house that day one glass at a time, never getting to the point that I was loaded and acting like an idiot. When darkness came, we turned on the Christmas lights for the first time and headed in for dinner. I set up the video camera on my phone and took a few pictures with the family during dinner. Memories were made. All that was left to do was to put the kids to bed, pour one more bourbon, and watch the end of the football game before I went to bed. It was the perfect ending to an even more perfect day!

I do not think that Jenny knows that Thanksgiving Day 2018 was a turning point for me. I woke up the next morning with a slight headache, but really not feeling too bad. I had paced myself the previous day. I went into the living room to have a cup of coffee and watch the news for a bit before everyone else woke up. I decided to flip through some of the Thanksgiving pictures on my phone. This is where it happened! I got a little nervous because I saw a picture of all of us wearing turkey hats and acting silly, but I did not remember taking it. I slid to the next ones, more pictures that I did not remember taking. I kept thinking to myself that I did not remember getting so drunk that I would not remember taking these pictures. Why could I not remember? I slid the pictures one more time to find the video. Ah! I do remember taking this video, well sort of. I remember taking it but I could not for the life of me remember what was on the video. I pressed play.

I watched the video a few times and was embarrassed with how I was acting. Although I was not doing anything wrong, not acting drunk, not slurring my speech or doing anything too out of the ordinary, I was not being me. I saw a totally different person, and I did not like him. This was the first real moment that I knew and accepted that I had a drinking problem. Now what was I going to do about it?

I made the decision that it was time for me to quit drinking for good. Although I was not ready to go to any official Alcoholics Anonymous meetings or go to a rehab facility, I was ready to tell Jenny that I felt as though I had a problem and needed her help to quit. I put down the bottle that day. With every fiber in my body, I fought this battle and finally felt as though I was winning.

VI. New Year's Eve Celebration

It was New Year's Eve, and I had officially made it thirty-seven days without a drink in my system! I had not even had a non-alcoholic beer, nothing! I felt great, but this accomplishment had not been easy. After a week or two, I started to have thoughts about this being a "forever" thing.

Forever is an extreme word. The longer I went without a drink, the more forever slipped away from my mind and the more I began to question myself. I repeatedly asked a number of questions in my mind during the thirty-seven days of sobriety: Is this really going to be forever? Am I never going to be able to drink again? What about on holidays? What about a glass of bourbon every now and then? Haven't I proved to myself that I can do this? Do I really have a problem if I can go without drinking for over a month? What if I gave myself limits now that I had made it this far? Could I start drinking a little now that I have this under control? Don't I owe it to myself to at least try a drink here or there? When should I have a congratulatory drink for making it over a month of sobriety? Surely I'll be able to have only one drink, won't I?

By the time my friend and I were headed to Charlotte, North Carolina for an Avett Brothers New Year's Eve concert, I had decided that I would have just one drink to celebrate and then not have another for a month or so. This sounded like a great plan; after all, I had come so far and deserved to light up my reward system with one drink. I remember that day very well.

We went to a restaurant for lunch, and I had decided that it was time for my reward. I had been anticipating this moment for a few weeks now. After eating lunch, I ordered a bourbon on the rocks. Looking at the glass sitting in front of me, I knew it was wrong. I contemplated leaving and not having even a sip of it, but once again, I was powerless over a drink. I took a sip and instantly remembered how much I loved every aspect of drinking. Well, every aspect except one--the guilt that I grew to associate with drinking alcohol. This time it was not the typical next-morning guilt that I was feeling. This guilt was different: I had let myself down and knew instantly that I had let Jenny down. I did not want to tell her that I had rewarded myself with a drink. The remainder of the evening was amazing. My friend and I went to the concert and rang in the New Year without having another drink, although I wanted another one badly when we got to the concert.

When we returned home, Jenny greeted me with a big hug and kiss and told me that she had missed me. Within two minutes she smiled and asked if I had decided to have a drink or not. Smiling, I said, "Yep, I sure did. I had one drink and didn't even want a second one." She said, "Oh. I really didn't expect you to do it, but ok." We did not talk much about it after that; we did not have to. Her face said it all. In our twelve years of marriage, I had never before seen such disappointment on her face. I knew that I had let her down. She had so much hope that I was really going to be successful this time. I could see that my action crushed her on the inside. I know that she did not mean to show this emotion, but it was there and something that I could not get off my mind for a while.

VII. The slow spiral to the bottom

Over the next month and a half, I slowly spiraled out of control and went from not drinking at all to not being able to control myself. It started slowly after getting home from the concert. I had a beer or a glass of bourbon on occasion, but then I noticed that "on occasion" turned into every night again. And "one every night" slowly evolved into me pouring a little more while people were not looking.

Within a month I was back to my heavy drinking pattern, but this time it seemed a little worse to me than ever. If you do not know much about alcoholism, it is a progressive disease. Typically for those who are true alcoholics, each time you fail at putting the drink down, the deeper you get into alcoholism. That was happening to me--I was spiraling out of control. I had never hidden bottles until this point in my alcoholism. By the end of January, I had a bottle of bourbon in the house, another in the garage, and still another in my music studio. None of them were hidden out of sight, but they were pretty much everywhere that I could get to them so that I could hide the amount of alcohol that I was drinking within a day. It even got to the point that I stopped at the store on the way home to buy two high alcohol content beers to drink when I got into our neighborhood.

I could not pretend that I did not have a problem at this point. I knew I did, but I did not want to give up the alcohol. I was doing things I had always said that I would not do, and I could not stop it. Nobody knew the reality of how bad it was because I hid it well. I would catch a quick high on my way home and would not have a drink for an hour or so. When the kids were in their bath, I poured a large glass of bourbon on the rocks to sip on until bedtime. To much of the outside world, having only one drink a night is no cause for alarm. Nobody else knew that I was drinking on my way home from work, and I was ok with that.

I remember those evening rides around the lake with a beer in my hand and how pitiful I felt doing this. I remember the shame I felt every night as I hid my drinking from my family. I remember thinking to myself, "Will there ever be a turning point? What is going to have to happen for me to make a change? Am I going to have to lose everything to open my eyes and quit?"

I got to a point where I was willing to accept the consequences of my addiction. I felt that there was really no way for me to quit drinking. I knew that there was no way out of this on my own, but I did not want to ask for help. I did not want to admit to anyone that I was spinning out of control. Little did I know, I had already hit rock bottom. I was blinded by the alcohol and did not know what was going to have to happen in order to change my life. What I did know was that I needed some kind of intervention to save my life, and I needed it quickly.

VIII. My Intervention

My intervention was not the typical intervention that is seen on television. You would think that Jenny's accident would wake me up and that my intervention would come immediately after; it did not. Instead, it came approximately ten days later. I am not going to get into the details of what took place during the ten days after Jenny's accident, but I self-medicated and did whatever I had to do to function through the day and get myself to sleep each night. My life was in complete disarray, and I wanted out. Jenny was in the hospital fighting for her life, and I was struggling to survive.

On day ten I was confronted by someone who laid it all out to me, not holding back anything and telling me things that I really needed to hear. The details of that conversation will stay private, but that person saved my life, and I will be forever grateful for that confrontation. I know it must not have been easy. When I went home from the hospital that morning, I had decisions to make, decisions that were going to change my life. I could either walk away from everything I had all for another drink, or I could face my problem and reach out for help. I chose to ask for help. I called the pastor of my church that same morning and told him that I needed to talk with him as soon as possible and that it was really important. We scheduled a time to meet after lunch.

VIII. The Decision

Although hesitant to do so, I met with my pastor exactly as planned. I showed up sober after making the decision about an hour earlier to go through the house and dump out every bottle of bourbon and every can of beer so that there would be no way for me to have a drink before our meeting.

I explained everything to him. I was broken, miserable, beaten down by all that had happened over the past ten days, and in the worst place I had ever been in my life. I did not care about myself and was struggling to function on a daily basis. My pastor told me that everything was going to be okay and that we were going to do whatever we needed to get me help if I was really ready for it. I told him I was, that I had to get help this time, and that I could not do it on my own. I added that I had been trying to do so unsuccessfully for the past year. Yes, I was ready for and desperately needed a change.

Together, we called Pine Grove Recovery Center. I was placed into an intensive outpatient program (IOP) for addiction. I was officially going to a rehabilitation clinic to get much-needed help for my addiction to alcohol.

IX. IOP Group – My fourth and final attempt

Walking into my IOP group for the first time was nerve wracking. I wondered, "Am I sure that I want to do this? Is this really what I need?" I did know that nothing else was working and that I was running out of chances. I was struggling to take care of my kids, my wife, and myself. I felt guilt, shame, and selfishness having to focus on rehabilitation while Jenny was fighting so hard inside that hospital. It took time to realize that it was ok to do seek help now and that I had to take care of myself if I ever wanted to be able to take care of them. I was sick, and I needed to get better.

I sat in a circle of chairs with about eight other people who were in there for treatment as well. Some of them had already been there for inpatient treatment and were now moved to this outpatient treatment for the next thirty days before being released. Only a few of us there that had not been to inpatient treatment prior to coming into this program. Our counselor came in and introduced herself to me. I was actually coming into the group about a week after they had already started it, so I was one of the new people to this group. I was hoping not to have to speak too much on this first day, not wanting these people to know too much about me just yet. I had not quite bought into to telling strangers, some of whom might know my family, friends, or coworkers, all of my deep dark secrets and what I had done in my alcoholic life. I mean, who in their right mind would want to divulge information that could potentially be used against you in so many different ways if it were to ever go outside the doors in that room? Needless to say, I was skeptical about this whole thing. I did not exactly trust this system at this point.

Our counselor welcomed me to the group and asked everyone to go around the room saying their first name, where they were from, and their drug of choice (DOC). When the first person said that her DOC was sex and love addiction, I immediately thought I was in the wrong place. "Wait, what?" I thought to myself. "I am here for alcohol addiction. Surely I am in the wrong place!" The next person identified her DOC as opioids. This time I thought, "Interesting. Closer to my addiction, but still not why I am here." The next girl stated that heroin was her DOC. At this point I realized that I was totally wrong about the stereotype I had played out in my mind.

I did not know that I would be in a room of people with different types of addictions; I figured I would be in a room with other alcoholics and had no idea how this was going to work or how they planned on "fixing" so many people with so many different addictions. As we continued around the room, I heard it all. Sex addiction, opioids, heroin, alcohol, and crystal meth seemed to be the main addictions, but many of us had also dabbled in other drugs like marijuana and cocaine at some point. Regardless, we were all powerless over our drug of choice.

I did not say too much that first day. I listened to them talk, and, believe me, this group talked. There were some impressive personalities in this room, but there was also something else that I found impressive about this group--not one of us was the stereotypical addict portrayed on television or in the movies. Those outlets portray addicts as dirty, washed-up people who live on the streets doing whatever they can to score their next fix. Not this group. It was filled with extremely smart people who, if seen outside this room, would never be suspected of having issues with addiction. We had stay-at-home wives, nurses, doctors, PhD's, college administrators, teachers, and the list goes on. Just about all of us were married and had children. Knowing this made me feel much better about where I was. By the end of the first day, I was actually looking forward to coming back and being part of this group. Over time I began to speak about my addiction issues and the things I did when I was in active addiction. To my surprise, I was not alone with some of the terrible choices I had made while drinking. I listened to others in my group tell the same stories. They had done many of the same things I had done when they were not sober.

I came up with a few interesting conclusions about addiction. It really does not matter what one's DOC is. The drug itself is not the problem. Instead, something in the brain that makes the person become addicted to that drug. The problem is an addiction. Our group's members came from different places and had different backgrounds, but we had some version of the same story. Ultimately, I realized that everyone in that room was there for the same reason: We were all addicts.

For the first time in my life as an addict, I felt as if I was not alone. I now had a group of people that I could talk to about anything, a group of people who really understood what I was going through. This group of "misfits" would eventually become people I still talk to almost daily to get through some days. I trust any of them with anything I have to say and know that they will not judge me. If I need to be talked down from taking that first sip again, all I have to do is reach out, and any of them will drop what they are doing to help me. I can honestly say that this group of people saved me from the chains of addiction that had weighed so heavily on me for as long as I can remember. I could not have done it and still could not do it without them in my life. These people whom I was so afraid to tell anything to probably know more of my deepest and darkest secrets than my closest friends know. And I trust them with that information. Sometimes I may think about taking that one sip, and that "stinking thinking" creeps back into my mind. However, this group jumps right in without judgment and does whatever they can to get me back on track as quickly as we possible.

Addiction is a dangerous disease. It takes only a moment of being off guard for it to slip in and take the addict back to that familiar place. If you have an addiction problem, like I do, a support system can be very helpful. In my experience the people in my support system are some of the most genuine people that I know, and I could not fight my addiction without them. If you are reading this and are afraid to get help and go to a rehab facility, don't be! Give it a try. You owe it to yourself!

The same goes for Alcoholics Anonymous. It proved to be a place where I was reassured that I was not the only person with these thoughts running through my head. For me, AA is a place to go let everything out without having to worry about the judgment or stigma attached to being an alcoholic. I can either talk or just listen. Sometimes just listening to the topics and the stories from others dealing with addiction is all I need at times. Knowing that I am not alone in my struggle to stay sober is a game changer, and I know that any time that I need someone to talk to or a place to go to see a friendly face, I can always go to a meeting. Being almost eight months sober as I write this book, I have not finished working my way through the twelve steps of AA. Some people think that I should have by now, but I have not quite gotten there. You know what? That is ok. Some people finish this process quickly; some take years to work the twelve steps. For me the process is not a race. I am taking my time, going to meetings when I can or need--sometimes multiple times a week and sometimes once a month. The wonderful thing about this program is that you do what works for you. Sometimes, I need it worse than other times. Sometimes I have more time on my hands to go to meetings.

We alcoholics and addicts still have to live our lives on a day-to-day basis. We have careers, families, and responsibilities that sometimes keep us from meetings. When we can catch a meeting, we do. When we cannot attend, we talk to others in our community who understand what we are going through. Whether that is our spouse, our sponsor, or a group of others with the same disease, we do anything we can to stay sober. My father has been sober for the past forty years, and he is one of the people that I message when I need to check myself when it comes to staying sober. I know that I can discuss anything with him at any time of the day. That is what we alcoholics do to stay sober, or we will never survive. We build our support system with people we can trust with anything, people who will not look down on us if we fail but who will do anything possible to pick us up and get us back on the right track.

I know the old cliché says, "one day at a time," but I am not a huge fan of that philosophy. Regarding alcohol, I prefer to think that I can drink anything I want tomorrow. Sometimes I look forward to getting to tomorrow so that I can have that drink then, but I have to stay sober today! I can worry about that drink tomorrow, but today, it is not an option. Thus far, this philosophy has worked for me: As long as I stay sober in the present, I will always be chasing tomorrow.

X. Life after rehab

For the better part of three months, I attended my IOP rehab group sessions as well as one-on-one sessions with my counselor. Discussions in these sessions were a life changer for me. I opened files in my brain that I had not realized impacted my drinking and that were factors as to why I drank so much. I never understood why I loved to drink and why I loved the high that alcohol gave me until I was in these sessions. I learned more about myself in three months than I had in years, some of which I was not happy with. More importantly, I also learned that it was necessary for me to unlock these feelings and face them if I ever wanted to heal from the mess they had made of my life.

In the weeks and months following my journey into sobriety, I have noticed amazing physical and mental changes. The most obvious is that I no longer wake up every morning feeling bad. I also no longer wake up feeling remorseful or wondering what I said or did the night before because of memory lapses that I formerly faced. Mentally, I am prepared to face each day with the clearest possible mind that I can have. I need that clear mind to take care of Ruby, Charlie and, most importantly, Jenny. They need me. Jenny needs her husband, and our children need their father. They need 100% of me, not that person who was simply just trying to survive.

I am not going to sugar coat this and say that I have been cured of this disease. I know that I will never be cured of my alcoholism and that I will struggle with the desire to have a drink for the rest of my life, but I am also well prepared to fight it until the end. Rehab gave me the tools to use, and it is now my turn to use them and live this life to the best of my ability. This does not mean that I will not stumble. This does not mean that it will all be unicorns and rainbows from here on out. What it does mean is that I have been given a second chance at life. To succeed, I need to look up and stay focused.

I now see my family and my life through a new set of eyes, eyes that actually pay attention to what kind of person I want my children to become. Eyes that no longer see that face of disappointment when Ruby asks me to do something and I say that I am too tired or that I do not feel well enough right now to do it. Most importantly, eyes that will no longer look at me with disappointment because I took another drink, but instead look at me with love and a thankful heart that she has her husband back. A sober husband with no thoughts of ever going back to the man he once was.

Seven

the sixth floor

Tuesday, February 19, 2019
6:09 P.M.

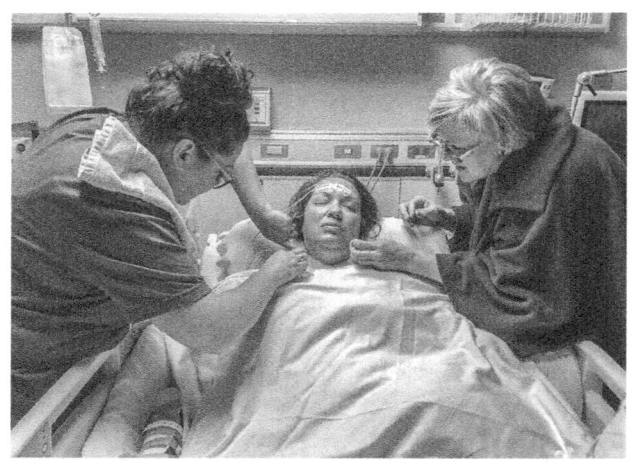

Back to the story... After three days in the ICU, Jenny was moved to a regular hospital room, where she would spend the next four weeks. A multitude of family and friends stepped in to take shifts. Jenny's mom typically spent the daytime hours with her while I took the kids to and from school and kept up the daily duties of the house, along with making phone calls to the insurance company, dealing with disability, paying bills, gathering information for our lawyer, trying to stop by the hospital to pop in for a minute to see her, and attending my IOP sessions three days a week. The days flew by, and just keeping up with our daily affairs became a full-time job.

In the evenings, friends came over to our home for about an hour to play with the kids so that I could head back to the hospital to watch over Jenny. When I got to the hospital, her mom headed back to take care of the kids and the house for the evening.

These times became bittersweet to me. I looked forward to seeing Jenny all day, but I also hated seeing her in so much pain, both physically and mentally. In the beginning, I could not show up to the hospital without self medicating to prepare myself for what I was about to deal with. At the time, selfishly I did not want to face what was happening. I did what I had to do at the time to be in that room with her and not explode into a hysterical fit of depression, anger, and emotion. Eventually, I faced all of this without self medication. When I did, I began seeing my wife differently and then realized that I was put in her life for this very moment. As the days went on and I dealt with the pressures sober, I became thankful that I had made the choice to get help. Had I not done so, I could have never been able to face this journey the way my wife needed me to do so.

We had our daily routine down to a science. Early each morning, one of Jenny's friends sat with her while I headed home to finish getting the kids ready for school and Jenny's mom returned for the day shift. Jenny's dad or her best friend took turns staying with her on weekends so that I could spend as much time with the kids as possible. Sometimes they stayed during the day so that I could stay with Jenny at night; other times, we switched it up so that I could spend the evening at home with the children. Although it was not an ideal way of living life for any of us, we did what we had to do in order to keep life as normal as possible for Ruby and Charlie. Without these friends, this set up would have been impossible, and our families will never forget the selflessness they demonstrated in our time of need.

These weekends were good for me. I spent quality time with Ruby and Charlie. Charlie had been weaning off breastfeeding but still had to be rocked to sleep every night, something Jenny typically did because she loved doing it. Evenings with our children became even more special to me: I learned much more about and bonded with Charlie and observed Ruby's amazing motherly instincts kick in. She went from being a six-year-old kindergartener to becoming a little girl who wanted to help with household and motherly duties. She made sure Charlie had everything he needed. It was instinctual for her to want to take care of both Charlie and me, and was simply beautiful to watch.

Getting to the hospital each day was like a "changing of the guard." I told Jenny's mom everything that had happened during the day and everything she needed to know about the kids. She told me everything that happened during the day with Jenny--what the doctors said when they came in, how her rehab went that day, how her pain was, and what medications she had taken. Our lists went on and on as though we were going through a checklist trying not to omit anything.

Jenny's time spent in this part of the hospital was not just to heal physically but also to start the rehabilitation process. A team of physical and occupational thera-pists made a schedule Jenny had to follow during the day. It consisted of moving on her own as much as she could, doing breathing exercises so that pneumonia would not set into her lungs, eating so that she could gain strength to heal, and her least favorite of the day…rehab. Her rehabilitation team came in for any-where from an hour to an hour and a half each day to get her started in recovery. They had to get her body moving so that she could relearn how to walk and live without the use of one of her arms. By the end of that first week, Jenny was sitting at the end of her bed and lying down. This usually simple action was a huge ac-complishment!

Over the next few weeks, Jenny's physical rehabilita-tion slowly progressed, and the pain in her arm slowly subsided. She became able to sit at the edge of her bed, then moved from standing and sitting with assis-tance to standing and sitting in a wheelchair with as-sistance. Next, she was able to use her foot to move the wheelchair across the floor, into the hallway, and back to the room. The last week or so, they needed to get her ready to be moved to the rehab floor. Before she could go there, she needed to be able to get dressed and walk a few steps with assistance--an extremely difficult task for her. Like the superhero she was quickly becoming, Jenny pushed through all of these tasks and hit every goal that had been laid out for her.

Evenings on the rehab floor were extremely difficult for the first few weeks. Jenny's mom and the people who visited throughout the day got to see how much progress she was making. By the time I got there later in the day, I got the side of her that few people saw--the side of a woman who was struggling with even wanting to be alive. Jenny was tired and in so much pain from her rehab and all the people visiting her that all she wanted to do was take her pain medication so that she could fall asleep. Speaking of pain medication, it took the doctors a while to get her mixture of medications right so that she was not feeling weird. At different times, the medication made her hallucinate, hear music playing that nobody else in the room heard, and talk about people who were not and had not been there at all. Her doctors finally got the mix of medications correct, and the weird events stopped.

During this time Mardi Gras had arrived, and Hattiesburg had its yearly parade. Ruby had been looking forward to our plans to go to it, and Jenny still wanted me to take her. I was able to do so because Jenny's mom brought Charlie to her home to take care of things there while Jenny's best friend from college stayed with her at the hospital. Ruby and I went to the parade with her friends so that she could have a little normalcy in her life, if only for an hour or so.

We were having a great time at the parade when I got a phone call. I was told that there had been a little set-back and that I needed to get back to the hospital as soon as I could: Jenny's arm had become infected. When I arrived, one of the doctors came in and said that this type of infection is fairly common with an am-putation of this type. With Jenny's arm as mangled as it was at the scene of the accident, dirt and other sub-stances could easily get into the open wound and cause infection. They were going to have to go into surgery that evening to "clean up" the infected area, hoping that it would not be too bad once they got in there. They did not want to have to take off any more of the arm than they had already because they were trying to save some of the arm below the elbow. Jenny's mother and father rushed back to the hospital as we prepared for yet another surgery.

As they were prepping Jenny, the surgeon came in and explained exactly what they were going to do and let us know the different things to prepare for after this surgery. He said that Jenny would likely be in pain after this one and that there might be either a vacuum or an open drip attached to her arm for a few days so that the area would not get infected again. He cautioned us that sometimes they have to do this three or four times when dealing with traumatic amputations like Jenny's. He assured us that they would take good care of her and that they would call the room when the surgery was complete. They rolled her back to the operating room, and we went back to her room to wait for the call.

About an hour passed and the phone rang. The surgeon reported,

"Mr. Maul, Jenny's surgery went great. Once we got inside, we saw that the infection was not as bad as we had expected. We cleaned up the area and did not have to take any more of her arm. We have to leave a small opening for it to drip so that it will stay clean. Hopefully no more infection will occur. After the wound heals without any more infection, we will be able to do the reconstruction surgery on her and get the site shaped up and complete. While I do not expect to have to do another infection clean up, we will keep an eye on it for the next few days to be sure."

This was great news: Because they did not have to put the vacuum in her arm, Jenny's pain would not be as severe.

For the next two weeks, we kept a close eye on Jenny's arm to make sure that it was healing correctly. Every time we took the bandage off, we all were a little nervous to see what it looked like. In the back of my mind, I was a little worried that she would need another surgery before we could do her reconstruction surgery, but everything healed extremely well. She was officially ready to have this arm shaped, and I could not have been any happier. This next step was something that Jenny had been awaiting, and, honestly, she needed a win for once.

Reconstructive surgery took place on March ninth. Jenny had been in the hospital for approximately three weeks, and we were all ready to get out of it and to start learning what our new lives would be like at home. Although we were still quite a long way from that, this surgery was a big step forward in making it possible. Jenny had to do it before she could be moved to the rehabilitation floor, and we were excited about it happening. Jenny was wheeled down to the surgery prep room yet again. This time, I had a little glimmer of hope that this might actually be the last surgery my wife would have to go through, hopefully forever.

An hour or so went by before we got a call saying that everything went well--Jenny was in recovery, and I would see her in her room within the next hour. When she returned, she was not quite awake, and I could see that something was attached to her arm--a vacuum to help flush out the arm as it healed for the next few days. This worried me a little, not because of the possibility of infection, but because I remembered what I had been told about the pain associated with these devices.

To say that the evening was tough is an understatement. Jenny was in much more pain than she had been thus far in this journey. She cried and moaned in excruciating pain all night, even when sleeping. The nurses did whatever they could to try to help her rest comfortably, but nothing worked. They gave her a pain pill and injected her PICC line with the opioid Dilaudid, an extremely strong but highly addictive drug. Jenny would have to take quite a bit of it over the next few weeks, but I could not worry about potential dependency at the time: Jenny's pain had to be controlled. The night went on and on. She was allowed to have the Dilaudid only once every four hours. The results of it were immediate; she was out of pain and asleep within a minute but still moaning. Within two hours, she was awake again in so much pain that she could hardly stand it. We counted down the minutes until she could have the next injection. This went on all night long and into the morning.

Over the next couple days, Jenny was not able to do any rehab. Focus was on the arm healing so that she could be moved to the rehab floor. As time passed, the pain subsided and the arm healed nicely. The vacuum line was removed within forty-eight hours. Three days after surgery, on the evening of March twelfth, Jenny was discharged from the sixth floor and admitted to the third floor, Rehabilitation. She was one step closer to coming home.

Eight

mental game

Saturday, February 23, 2019
12:27 PM

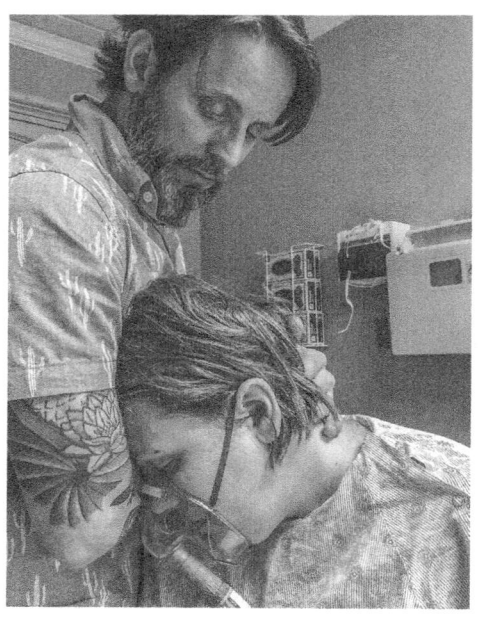

I remember worrying about Jenny's mental spirit a few times. I felt as though this beautiful strong-willed woman was beginning to slip away from everyone and wanting to give up on life. God, who could blame her! Knowing what she had been through and what she was currently going through would have driven most people to give up on life long before this. The fact that she needed assistance from another person for almost any task took a toll on her. Jenny realized that simple tasks we all take for granted, tasks like feeding herself or using the restroom, were taxing on her body.

When Jenny had to get out of bed, multiple people were needed. I had to help her maneuver to sit up, unplug her legs from a machine that helped with her circulation, and then call in nurses to help lift her legs an inch off the bed so that we could rotate her enough to lower her legs slowly onto the floor. Then someone had to hold her back up and slowly raise her enough to sit at the end of the bed. A nursing assistant then moved around to the front of her and let her hug his or her neck so that they could help her up. She moaned in agony each time that we moved her, and I cannot begin to imagine the amount of pain she felt during these times. This long, painful process stripped away Jenny's independence, freedom, and dignity.

During one of the first nights on the sixth floor, I became particularly concerned. Jenny asked the nurses to let it be just the two of us in her room for a while. As she sat crying, I just held her. She was praying and crying out to Jesus for help. At one point she screamed, not in pain, but in anger and frustration. I knew that there was absolutely nothing I could say to make it better. My heart was aching for her, yet all I could do was hold her. She was at a breaking point and I understood why. I did not say a word. None were needed. I just held her.

Another worrisome situation was that Jenny had not seen the Ruby and Charlie up to this point, nor had she wanted to do so. Every time I mentioned it, she said, "I do not want them to see me like this. I am not ready yet." I did not want to push the issue, but almost two weeks had passed since the accident, and she had not seen our children except in pictures. Her progress was at a standstill, and she was slipping in and out of major anger and depression. One of the nurses pulled me aside one evening and asked why she had not seen her kids yet. I told her that Jenny did not want them to see her in this state. The nurse said, "It would be good for her and the children. She needs to see those children so that it will give her something to look forward to. Maybe you could talk her into at least doing FaceTime with them?" I wholeheartedly agreed with her and immediately talked to Jenny about it. She was willing, and we set up a time to FaceTime that evening.

Ruby was so excited to see her mommy, even if on FaceTime. Jenny cried when she saw Ruby and Charlie and heard their voices. It was beautiful, but I could see a mother's heart breaking. She missed them both so much and was angry that someone had taken away these moments from her children. She later told me that she felt like she was missing so much of their lives and that she wondered why she was even still here. I told her that I did not know why she was spared from this horrific wreck but knew that she was still on this earth for a reason. For now, I needed her to focus on being here for them. The real reason for her still being here would be seen in time, but for now she needed to concentrate on getting better for her children and for me, because selfishly, I needed her. A few days later, my wife asked me to bring our children to see her at the hospital.

I was excited and nervous the day I finally got to bring the children to see Jenny and can only imagine that Jenny was feeling the same emotions. The last time she had seen them was when people were getting them out of the car at the scene of the accident. I remember getting off the elevator and rounding the corner to Jenny's room. The same nurse who had talked to me in the hallway a few nights ago was at the nurse's station. We looked at each other, and she had the biggest smile on her face when she saw the children. I introduced Ruby and Charlie to her and told them that this was one of the nurses taking care of their mommy. The nurse looked at me, smiled, and did not have to say anything. I knew what she was thinking and I agreed: This was going to be a special moment for all of us.

I opened the door, and we walked into the room. Jenny was with her parents waiting on us. Lying in her bed with the back inclined upward just a bit so that she would be able to see them better, she had the biggest smile on her face, and tears of joy started to flow. Her eyes lit up with the love that she has for our children. Ruby asked why Mommy was crying, and I told her Mommy was happy to see her. I told Ruby that she could hug her, but she needed to be careful not to be too rough because Mommy was still in a lot of pain. Ruby went over to Jenny, hugged her, and said, "I love you and I miss you, Mommy." As they embraced for the first time since the night of the accident, Jenny's emotions took over. She held Ruby as though she never wanted to let go of her again.

At first, I kept Charlie in my arms because we were a little concerned that he would want to jump out to Jenny upon seeing her. I slowly walked him over toward her. He was timid as Jenny spoke to him. I had been a little nervous about his first reaction and had hoped that he would be excited to see her so that she did not think he had forgotten about her. We did not need any setbacks. I needed her seeing our children make her will to live stronger. As Jenny talked to Charlie, he smiled. As we got closer to her, he leaned forward and I laid him on her chest. He did not go crazy trying to hug her or flail around on her as I had expected. Instead, he smiled and gently laid his head onto her chest as though he knew that she was hurting and just wanted to hug and love on his mommy. His embrace with her seemed to communicate, "You are going to be okay, Mommy."

We stayed for about an hour--just enough time for the three of them to talk, hug, and enjoy each other's company. Ruby had questions about Jenny's arm, and we were honest with her about what had happened. She seemed a little nervous to see Jenny missing part of her arm, but she looked at Jenny and said, "It will be ok, Mommy." I watched in amazement of how she handled this situation at the young age of six. Ruby has that special spirit that Jenny has, that spirit of love that so many people talk about when they meet Jenny. Both mother and daughter care about and genuinely love people, and it is obvious upon meeting them.

This day was exactly what Jenny needed; in fact, it was exactly what we all needed. Jenny was not the only one struggling to survive and in need of some hope that day. We all needed that moment. This first of many trips to see Jenny at the hospital was a spiritual moment.

Jenny's anger and emotions came in waves. Some days I got to the hospital and thought that we had hit a turning point because she was in such a good mood. Other days, I arrived and could tell that she had had a rough day. She was depressed, her body hurt, and I knew that she had worries on her mind. Some nights we talked about it; other nights, Jenny just went to sleep.

I remember very well one night when Jenny cried quite a bit and could tell that she had been crying on and off all day. When I asked what was bothering her, she told me that she could not get Ruby off her mind. Jenny had realized that day that she was not going to be able to do some of the things she had previously done and loved doing for Ruby. The one thing really bothering her was the fact that she would not be able to do Ruby's hair with only one hand. This was a huge deal for Jenny. When she was a girl about Ruby's age, Jenny did her baby doll's hair all the time. She had once told me that she dreamed of having a little girl so that she could play with and be able to style her hair.

Before the accident, Jenny had done Ruby's hair for school every morning, and I could see the frustration in her face about the thought of not being able to do so anymore. This is one example of thoughts that arose in her mind, wondering how her life could ever be the same with one arm. Spoiler alert...Jenny can now put Ruby's hair into different styles and ponytails using one hand and her mouth. It is amazing to see how she has persevered over the past eight months.

Rumors started circulating about the status of the other driver. Out of respect for his family, I am not going to write much about it except to say that he did pass after a few weeks. Worried about how this news was going to affect Jenny, I decided she did not need to know just yet and refrained from telling her. She was progressing well with her recovery at this point, and I did not want to do anything to jeopardize that progress.

I got a call from Jenny's friend one afternoon saying that she had told Jenny about the other driver passing away. Jenny was asking about him, and her friend could not lie to her about it. Although I understood where she was coming from, I was not exactly happy that this was the way Jenny found out about him. I felt that this was something I needed to tell her, but I also know how hard it is to lie to Jenny. She can read people well, especially people that she really cares about. She would have known something was up if her friend had told her that she did not know anything. When I got to the hospital that evening, Jenny and I talked a little about it. She did not cry much; instead, she shook her head and said, "Why did he get the easy way out of this?"

This was one of those moments that required no response. We did not talk about it after that. Sometimes you listen to someone to listen and not to answer back. This part of our journey was over, and it was time to move on. To this day, we still do not talk much about how she felt and feels about it. This one is between her and God, and I am ok with that. Some things about all of this are simply not any of my business, and this seems to be one of them.

In different ways, the time spent in the hospital wreaked havoc on our mental states, but it was necessary. It was necessary for us. We had to go through all of this as part of the grieving, healing, and growing process. It was just the beginning of the fight we endured and still endure almost a year later. Will this fight ever be over? I do not think so. I think that in time it will get easier, but there will probably always be a little inner struggle lingering.

I have forgiven the other person for this situation. I think that we both have, but I think that there will always be times of anger for me. How I react to these moments will either take me back to that place of depression that I often slip into about all of this or I will use these moments to grow. I like to think that it will be the latter of the two, but I am not going to fool myself. As with my alcoholism, this situation is a mental struggle from which I will be rehabilitating for the rest of my life. It will force me to grow into a stronger person over time.

I cannot speak for Jenny on this matter. She has to live with so many thoughts I will never know. My prayer is that she will keep the positive spirit she has and will rise up from the ashes. I have no doubt that she will do just that. My wife is the strongest, most forgiving person I have ever known.

Nine

visitors

Sunday, March 3, 2019
7:38 P.M.

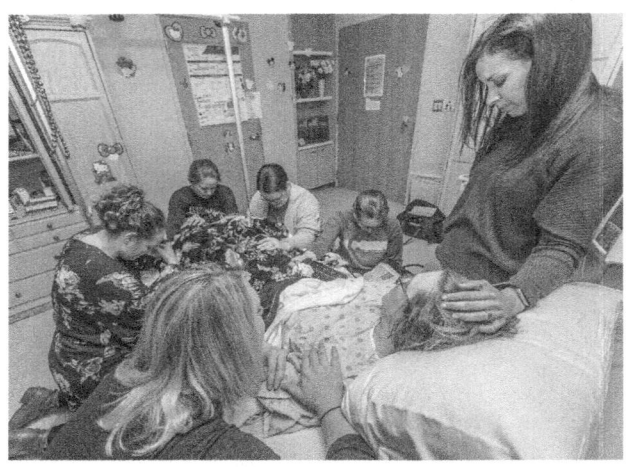

Over the approximately eight weeks that Jenny spent in the hospital, she had a number of visitors. Of course, our close friends and family came to visit daily. What we did not expect was the number of other people who showed up. Some came in once to say hi and see how Jenny was doing; others popped in from time to time to check in on her and try to keep her spirits up. Visitors included people whom we knew well, people we did not know at all who were traveling through on their way to another Avett Brothers concert, old friends from her grade school days, college friends, coworkers, and the list goes on and on. Two specific visitations were extremely meaningful to both Jenny and me.

I was present for the first one, and it was simply beautiful to watch. We live in a neighborhood where we have become close to a particular group of friends. There are many whom we consider friends, but this group is special--that group of people you know you can count on for anything. If you do not have a group of friends like this, you are missing out because it is such a special gift. We could not have made it through all of this without these women.

One of them women is also Jenny's OB-GYN and the person who brought our children into the world. She is also one of the most spiritual women whom I know. On one of the many days that she came by to check in on Jenny, she pulled me aside and asked, "Do you think Jenny would be ok with me getting all of the wives together to come pray for her one evening?" I said, "Absolutely! She would love that. She needs to see some familiar faces. I know that doing so would be good for her." She went on her way, and within a few days she had her idea set up. I did not tell Jenny that it was going to happen, but I went to the hospital that evening with my camera so that I could capture this moment. I just knew that it was going to be special.

The time came and there was a knock on the door. As I opened the door, these women filed in one at a time. Jenny's eyes lit up and a big smile came across her face, not expecting to see these five women walk in to see her all at one time. As they hugged Jenny and told her that they were there to pray for her, she started to cry. Each of them knelt down and took their place by her side around the bed. Laying their hands on her, the first one started reading a passage from the Bible about God calling Martha's brother Lazarus out of the grave, John 11:21-44. This was her way of telling Jenny to take off her grave clothes and come out of the grave of darkness. After she read the passage, each of the other four took her turn saying her own special prayer for Jenny as we were all trying to hold back tears.

Watching this interaction take place was absolutely beautiful! No words can express how much this prayer session meant, and I realized what a blessing it is to have such a group of selfless friends! While there was not a dry eye in the room, there was a presence of peace and calming, if only for a minute. At this very moment Jenny was healed and there was no pain in our hearts. I stepped out for a while to let them all have time with her and to take in and process the outpouring of love and support that had taken place. I will never forget this night in the hospital, and Jenny feels the same way.

There was a time that I thought Jenny was about to give up. She went in and out of depressive states, and her crying spells became more and more frequent. When I arrived at the hospital every night, Jenny wanted to talk less and less. Instead, she lay there crying and was ready to take her medication so that she could sleep. I was worried that she was going to slip into a severe depression and that I was going to lose her. The mind is a crazy place that can take over and lock you into some scary places, places that I have been, and they are not fun. It takes a while to climb out of those places; some never return no matter how hard they try to escape. I worried that this was happening to my wife, and I could not have blamed her. If it had been me in that bed, I would have given up in the ICU and most likely never returned.

The second noteworthy visitation occurred when I was not present. I hope that I get it right, based on what Jenny told me. It snapped her out of the depression that was setting in and reset her mind, body and soul and goes something like this. Jenny works at a school in Columbia, Mississippi. She had become close to a number of coworkers, but there has always been one constant there since she started. This woman and her husband had become more like family to Jenny, not just someone she works with. One day this friend's husband got word of the struggle that Jenny was having. He also knew about my battle with sobriety. Jenny did not know that I was in my own rehab at this time. We had decided to keep that a secret until she was strong enough to deal with the fact that I had relapsed and needed to take care of myself. To this day, I do not know if part of the reason for him visiting was that he suspected my struggle flaring up. Being a recovering alcoholic himself, I like to think that he was there not only for Jenny but for our family and that he had come to pray for all of us to have strength in the wars that were being waged against us.

One day, this man and his friend burst into Jenny's room. She said that they had a look in their eyes that was different from any other time they had come in. They walked up to her in the bed and said that they were there for one reason, to pray for her, and began doing so. I do not know exactly what they prayed for; that is between them, Jenny and God, but I do know that something significant happened to Jenny that day. She told me that as they had their heads down and were praying for her, she opened her eyes to a bright white light that looked as though it was coming directly from her chest. She said that this spiritual moment resulted in her knowing that she was going to be okay from that point on. Some readers may not believe what she says she witnessed, but I do. One thing I know about my wife is that she is not going to make up something that did not happen. As crazy as it may sound, I believe that there was a spiritual awakening in Jenny's hospital room that night. I have witnessed that awakening with the love and compassion that my wife has to this day. She is a different person because of this incident. She is renewed and reborn, and I have to believe that this day was part of that rebirth.

Jenny told me that when they were finished praying, the one gentleman looked at his friend and said, "Is there anything else that you need to say?" She said that he looked around the room and then looked at her and said, "I feel the spirit here today. God is telling me, when you are feeling down, you look up!" They then turned around and left. Jenny has told me many times that this was an enlightening moment for her, and I have to agree. Her attitude changed, and she began to grow stronger. Her willpower and motivation seemed to get stronger instantly.

I do not know if you, the reader, believe in God or another higher power out there. If you do not, I ask you to start searching for your purpose on this earth. I have witnessed so much over the past eight months that I cannot and will not try to explain. These things all lead me to believe that there has to be some higher power out there guiding me through my journey on this planet, and, for me, that higher power is God. If you have not found your purpose in life or that guiding power, I urge you to take some time to search inside yourself and find your true meaning. There is no denying the healing powers have been used on our family. I have three, make that four reasons, to believe that there is something greater than myself out there directing my life. I have two children who only had minor scratches walk away from an accident that should have taken their lives. I have a wife who, by all medical accounts, should not be here; even doctors are in amazement at her recovery. And I have myself. I have a second chance at this life. A new clean and sober chance to be a husband and father to my family. I have a new meaning--to help others struggling with depression and addiction. I could not have done and know that I will not be able to continue to accomplish these things without my higher power, so I thank you, God! Thank you for waiting on me, and thank you for showing me that your timing is perfect!

Ten

the third floor

Friday, March 15, 2019
11:51 A.M.

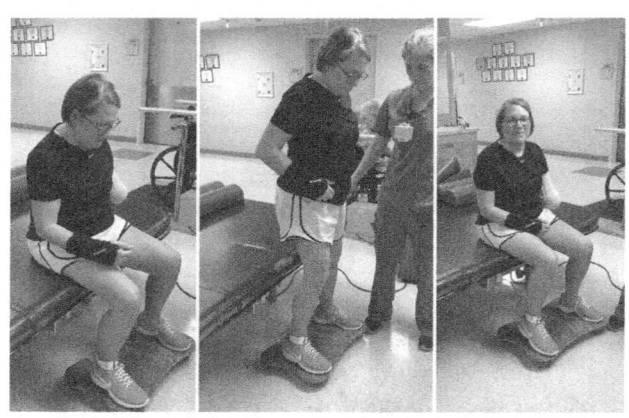

Nervousness and fear were what I saw in Jenny's eyes as we made our way out of the comforts of the room on the sixth floor to advance to the rehabilitation floor. It was a bittersweet moment. We had become familiar with this oversized hospital room and the staff that had been taking care of Jenny. To us, these people had become more than just nurses and caregivers; over the past month, they had become part of our family. They had gone above and beyond to make both Jenny and me comfortable. They had shared her triumphs, her pains, and her fears with her on a daily basis. They had even shared our twelfth anniversary with us on this floor! Jenny was not ready to leave these people that she had come to trust so much, but it was time to move on to the floor that would ultimately get Jenny home to our family again and one step closer to freedom. Although the rehab floor was not going to be easy, Jenny was as prepared as she could have been.

We made our way through many hallways with what seemed to be a never-ending maze of turns until we came to a large door. The aide who was rolling Jenny's bed from the sixth floor to the third floor stopped and pressed a large silver button. The door swung open to show us a large room full of different apparatuses used to assist in rehabilitation. People in wheelchairs were hanging out in the hallways. We rolled all the way to the end of the hall and went into the last room on the left, Jenny's new room, and immediately noticed that it was much smaller and more confining. Also, instead of the nice view of Hattiesburg that we had on the sixth floor, we now looked out the window to see the back of the building next to us. Needless to say, the first impression was not good one, making it more difficult for Jenny to buy in to this move. Tears started to stream from her eyes. She was struggling with this transition and wanted to go back to the comfort and familiarity of the sixth floor.

The certified nursing assistant came in and introduced herself to us. She was a short, spunky little thing who had a voice and persona that lit up the room. She immediately noticed that Jenny was upset and did everything she could to make this move easier for her. She took her time with Jenny, explaining in detail exactly what to expect while on this floor. She reassured Jenny that she would be taken care of and told us both not to hesitate in asking questions. This woman did everything she could to make Jenny and me feel more comfortable and to help us make this transition a little less stressful. When she left, we sat there looking at each other.

I knew that my wife was sad and scared. I told Jenny that I knew that this room was smaller and that she wanted to be back in her other room but that I needed her to try to think about this transition as a positive thing, a step closer to coming home. It meant that she had been healing and that her body was getting stronger. I reminded her that she had already won three major battles: She had made it from the scene of a near fatal accident to the ICU, had been moved from the ICU after only three days, and now had been moved to the rehabilitation floor. I reminded her that the ultimate goal at the beginning of this journey had been to get to this floor if she ever wanted to make it home. Oh, and all of this had been accomplished in less than a month! Nobody else had expected such progress, but they did not know my wife the way that I know her!

Rehabilitation back on the sixth floor was interesting. Jenny was still in so much pain when it began that her goals were small. It started with sitting up in her bed. After a few days, she progressed to sitting up in her bed and putting her feet on the ground for a few minutes. Eventually she had to learn how to get herself dressed with the use of one arm while enduring so much pain. Also during the sixth floor physical therapy, Jenny went from sitting in a wheelchair and pushing herself around the floor with one foot to standing and walking. Although these seemingly small tasks were done with assistance, they were all huge accomplishments. The rehab team there had come three to four times a week to work with her. Each session had left Jenny extremely sore and worn out. She slept the rest of the day, which was good because her body needed the rest so that it could heal and get stronger.

Thinking back, it still amazes me that, in just under one month of this accident, Jenny went from me helping her lift her left knee up about one inch to being able to stand and walk with assistance from her physical therapists. The combination of the human body doing what it does to heal, the resilience of her mind, and her never-ending spirit to survive amazed me daily. Jenny did not see the progress that she was making, but everyone else did. Personally, I could not wait to see what she would be able to do on this floor and just knew that she would own this floor once she was ready to start.

That same night of our arrival on the rehabilitation floor, we learned what Jenny's daily schedule would involve. It was quite a bit more intensive than that of the sixth floor. We had heard a little about what to expect prior to being moved down here, but we did not realize that it would be more like a job for her. Thinking about it, it was a job. Jenny only had one job to worry about, and that was to get home. Her new daily schedule had been set:

Breakfast
Occupational Therapy
Physical Therapy
Lunch
Pain medication and sleep
Dinner
Visitation hours *(no later than 9:00 P.M.)*

Not surprisingly, the days were packed for all of us, but our schedule worked out well. The family and friend routine stayed the same as it was on the sixth floor. Jenny's mom spent the day watching her rehab and updating me with any progress that occurred. I took the kids to school, went to my own rehab and AA meetings, and then went back to school to pick up our children. Jenny and I were both rehabilitating; it had become a team effort, and we were not going to lose our way. Her mom and I traded places around dinner time, and typically a few visitors were at the hospital when I arrived. At nine o'clock when all visitors were asked to leave, Jenny and I were able to spend quiet time together.

These became special times to me. There were moments of laughter as we watched Steve Harvey on

Family Feud. There were moments of tears as we discussed everything that had taken place and tried to figure out what this new life would be like. There were times when I loaded Jenny into her wheelchair and simply enjoyed the quietness of our walks. We roamed the hospital, me pushing her in her wheelchair, getting lost, and trying to find our way back to her room. Once, we ended up on the maternity floor and, hearing babies crying, reminisced about our two babies being born in this hospital. Their births were the last two times we had been and were two of the happiest moments of our lives. I could not help but think about how lucky I was to still have my two children and my wife in my life. I cannot speak for Jenny because we did not talk about it much, but I am sure that some of these same thoughts were going through her mind as we walked that floor trying to remember which rooms our babies were born in. Some of the most special moments we shared occurred when we did not say anything at all, moments when words could not express the way that either of us was feeling. The touch of Jenny's hand in mine and the look in her eyes spoke more than any words could have. These were reassuring moments that let me know that everything was going to be fine.

I will never forget these moments together. Moments of sadness and anger. Moments of happiness, joy and accomplishment. Moments of wonder and worry. Moments of excitement and pain. Moments of forgiveness and grieving. Most significantly, moments of relearning, forgiving, and reconnecting with the things that truly were important. We were both going through a rehabilitation of our minds, bodies, spirit, and marriage.

Jenny's rehabilitation consisted of two different sessions, the first being that of occupational therapy. According to Google, the definition of occupational therapy is "a form of therapy for those recuperating from physical or mental illness that encourages rehabilitation through the performance of activities required in daily life." That is exactly what these therapists did to help Jenny, who practiced everything in these sessions. Their goal was to try to determine how she would adjust to life with the use of only one arm. She practiced everything with these therapists: how to brush her teeth, get dressed, open bags and jars, and numerous everyday tasks. Their goal was to make Jenny feel as comfortable with one arm as possible before she returned home.

The physical therapy sessions made Jenny sore and tired every day. She did not look forward to them but knew that it was important for her to get strong enough to regain the freedom that had been taken from her. These therapists pushed her as far as they could each day and worked miracles on her. They even built her a special walker so that she could walk unassisted for the first time since the accident. This device became what she needed to be able to walk for the next few months.

Sadly, I do not know many details about Jenny's time in rehab as this took place during the day while I was also going through my own rehab at the time. Thankfully, Jenny's mom was present for these sessions and sent me videos of her accomplishments. I had to focus on myself and our children during the day, and Jenny understood that. You see, it was not until Jenny was on this floor that we started to talk a little about my time in rehab and the struggles that I was facing in the outside world. We did not speak much about it, she just let me know that she was proud of me for taking this life changing step. These moments were their moments, just like the evenings were our moments. These videos are all that I have for the daytime memories of Jenny being in rehab, but it is symbolic to me that we were both going through rehab at the same time. In different ways, we were both fighting to become stronger for each other and for our children. I will never forget two particular videos that Jenny's mom sent because they are defining moments in Jenny's recovery.

One video took place during physical therapy on March 15, 2019, exactly one day before the one-month anniversary of the accident that confined her to lying in a bed and took away all the dignity and freedom she had of being able to do anything without assistance from another person. On that day at exactly 11:51 A.M. and against all odds, Jenny stood up on her own for the first time since February 16, 2019! The video brought tears to my eyes. It was a short moment, but seeing her little crooked smile at the end of the video was the most beautiful thing I had ever seen. I was so proud of how far she had come in such a short amount of time and knew that this was only the beginning of Jenny's return to an independent life.

The second video took place during an occupational therapy session. This one was funny to watch. If you know my wife, you know that she absolutely loves to clean. I know, it is weird, but she does. She loves to have a clean house and feels a sense of accomplishment when she has one. She may be the only person I have ever met who thoroughly enjoys cleaning. I received this video and saw her standing with an unfolded towel in her hand. Not knowing what this video was going to be about, I pressed play and stood in amazement as I watched her fold a towel with one hand. Let me say that again: She folded a towel with one hand. Take a second to grab a towel and try to figure that out. I watched that video over and over and could hear the joy in her voice as she said, "Ain't nobody got time for these towels not to be folded correctly!" Then she smiled and laughed and added, "And I'm going to figure out how to fold a fitted sheet, too!" I have no doubt in my mind that she will.

During these times spent in the rehab room, Jenny noticed a fake car in the hallway and wondered if she was going to have to practice getting into and out of it. We had talked a few times about the fact that she was going to have to get into a car to go home soon. Each time, Jenny became nervous. Fear and PTSD from the accident were going to make it difficult for her to want to be a passenger in a car. At this point, I did not know if she would ever be able to drive a car again.

The rehab team decided that it was time to practice getting in the fake car because she and her mom needed to know how to load her into and get her out of the car safely when the time came. Reluctantly, Jenny got into the car and memories of the accident flooded in immediately. She broke into tears, the first of many times that she had to face the fear of being in a car. I can only imagine how difficult this moment must have been for her after what she had experienced.

The next day, Jenny's rehabilitation team met to discuss her progress after having spent one week in the rehabilitation unit. As is standard, the team meets once a week to discuss patient activity and come up with a plan for the upcoming week. The team finished their deliberation, and a nurse came in to inform us that the rehabilitation team was extremely impressed with the progress that she had made. In fact, Jenny would be allowed to go home by the end of the week. Needless to say, we were excited! However, there was still one task needed to get her ready for that day-- They wanted to practice getting in and out of the exact car that would be taking Jenny home from the hospital so that there would be no surprises on the day that she was released.

Three days before she was set to go home, her therapists put Jenny into her wheelchair and headed out to the parking garage. Jenny's mom was going to be driving her home from the hospital so that I could pick up the children from school and daycare that day. Wanting to surprise them when the time came, we were not planning to tell them about the possibility of Jenny coming home getting so close. Making their way into the parking garage, Jenny sat in her wheelchair with her physical therapists while her mom left to take her car around to the loading area. Jenny describes this moment to me as absolutely terrifying to her. She said that as she saw her mom pulling around the corner and driving toward her, she started to get nervous, noticed her heart racing, had difficulty breathing and started sweating. She was having a panic attack just seeing the car moving toward her. At the time, Jenny did not know what was going on, only that she was terrified of the car and could not stop picturing moments from the accident. She tried to calm her nerves as they loaded her into and back out of the car. She had done it! She had pushed through the panic attack and faced a fear that I likely would not have been ready to face. Jenny had won that battle that day and was officially ready to go home. Two full months had passed since Jenny had been flown to the hospital clinging on to what life was left in her body. Medical personnel expected her to be there a minimum of four months. Upon entering the rehab floor, she was told that she should expect to spend the next twenty-one days there. These people did not know the drive Jenny has within her. Defying all odds, after two months in the hospital with twelve days on the rehab floor, Jenny was headed home!

Eleven

home

Friday, March 22, 2019
3:42 P.M.

"After all that time, everyone longing for me to come home, leaving my new safe place where everyone knew me as the broken, one-armed me, the process of leaving that place seemed uneventful--until my family walked in the door. That's what I'll always remember," says Jenny about the day that she was to come home.

Jenny's mom was in charge of getting her into the car and driving her home. We were all a little nervous about this transition, probably more nervous than Jenny was. We did not know what to expect, but we were prepared for the worst. Would she freeze up and not want to get into the car? Would she have a nervous breakdown? Would she start crying?

The plan was for her mom to get Jenny home and comfortable while I was out picking up the children from school and daycare. Jenny's mom drove her home that morning, and I was excited to be getting my wife back where she belonged. I knew that it was not going to be easy for any of us to adjust to this new way of life, but I was ready to face it head on.

I had never asked about the ride home until now but feel that Jenny's response is something that needs to be told. She said, "The ride home was a happy time for my mom, but I was indifferent. I was not sure how to feel. I did not know how to be home and how to be taken care of; I had taken care of everyone." That is all that she knew of home life. When she first said this, I was caught a little off guard. I had always thought that I pulled my fair share of the weight around the house, but then I started to think about what she had said.

Looking back now through sober eyes, I agree with her one hundred percent. Jenny did take care of everyone. While I was there and did my fair share of the chores and being a father to our children, I was not always present in the daily grind of being a husband first and a father second. Instead, I had been too worried about when and where I was going to get my next drink. Subconsciously, my mind was saturated with liquor. Even when I was not drinking, I was not clear-headed. Without realizing the control that this substance had over me, I had been going through the day thinking that I was providing for my family and taking care of them. In reality, I was walking through life under the guidance of a substance. Jenny was correct: she had been the one taking care of our kids, the house, and me. On the outside it looked like our marriage was a fairy tale and that we had everything anyone would ever want, but that was a lie.

I now realize that the only thing that Jenny wanted and needed was me. Not just a part of me, and definitely not this part of me that I always fooled myself was normal, but all of me. She needed the man that she married, not the man who had slowly been drowning himself in a bottle just to feel normal. I still have to work on that man. I still have to chase him, and I will be chasing this person for the rest of my life. I owe that to her and to our children.

At this point, I had been sober for twenty-three days and felt great. I knew that it was still early in my sobriety and that having Jenny home would provide new stressors that would test my sobriety. I did not want to slip back to the person I had been twenty-three days ago and was thankful that I still had two months left to attend my rehab program. Going to rehab and attending AA meetings would become my "safe place" over the next few months--my place to be free from everything and everyone, if only for a while. I knew that I would need something to help take my mind off what was taking place at home and that coming to these meetings would be my way of letting go of everything and focusing on myself for a few hours a day. If I wanted to stay sober throughout our adjustment, I knew that I would need this escape, these places, and, most importantly, these people who did not judge me for anything I was feeling or needing to get out into the open.

I picked up Ruby from school a little early that day because the excitement had been building inside me like a kid at Christmas. We decided not to tell Ruby beforehand that Jenny coming home that day. We wanted it to be a surprise. After getting Ruby, I made my way to pick up Charlie from daycare and started our twenty-minute drive home.

For Ruby and Charlie, it was like any other day. Ruby was doing her typical play-by-play about everything that happened in a kindergartner's daily life--coloring, running, playing, lunch, learning to read, math, the usual daily grind of a six-year-old. Charlie sat in his car seat living the good life while listening intently to his sister discuss the important happenings of the day. He held on to every word as he sat with his daily after-daycare snack and drink in hand. He was quiet, not making any noise except to let me know that he was finished with his snack and wanted another one. I tried to listen to everything that Ruby said, but was too excited to soak any of it in. I was doing everything I could not to ruin the surprise. We finally pulled up to the house, and Ruby noticed that there were two cars there. She knew something was going on, but what?

Before we went into the house, I told her that I had a little surprise for her and that she needed to wait for me to get Charlie out the car before rushing inside. She was excited. This girl loves a surprise. We walked up to the front door, and I told Ruby to open it for me since my hands were full with Charlie and her backpack. She opened the door and inside was Jenny, sitting in her rocker with a big smile on her face. Ruby yelled out, "MOMMY!" and ran over to hug her. Their embrace lasted forever. Both of them cried as they held each other.

For Jenny, this must have been a happy and emotional moment. She had set out on a typical afternoon drive to see her parents over two months ago and had not been back home with her family until today. Charlie and I walked over to Jenny. I hugged and kissed her and said, "Welcome home! We've missed you!" Charlie wanted to be with his mommy, but I had to be cautious for him not to jump on her just yet. We knew that it was going to be tough on her not to be able to hold him for a while. The reconstruction on the amputated arm was still healing, and the broken bone in her right wrist was going to make it difficult for her to hold him. For now, I would have to hold him and help her maneuver him so that she could feel safe while holding him. When she did finally get situated enough to hold her little man, her emotions took over again and she wept.

Jenny talks often about being angry for having to miss so much time with our children. She describes it as feeling as though she had been robbed from watching them grow for the past few months. But at that moment of reunion at home, Charlie took all that worry away when he reached out for his mommy and acted as though she had been there the entire time. He cuddled up to his mother just like he had the last time he was with her in this house a few months ago. Jenny needed this therapy. She needed to be home with her family, and we needed her home, too.

Over the next few days, a flood of emotions and people went through our house. Depression, fear, anger, anxiety, family, friends, neighbors, people from our church and community bringing us food. Everyone wanted to visit Jenny, but they also knew that we would need some space. It was a difficult time for me, because I was doing everything I could to protect my wife and myself from the emotional rollercoaster that we were both on. I remember many days leaving the house to take the kids to school and go to my rehab session. When I returned, Jenny was often on the couch watching video after video of other amputees' stories or talking with visitors. Most people did not stay long, just wanting to say hi, letting us know that they were thinking about us, and praying for us. I did my best to try to make her feel comfortable and to make our guests feel welcome, but it was difficult. We were tired, and we were still fighting the fight. I still had sleepless nights, waking up at any little noise that she made. Sometimes I thought that all of this was helping in her healing process, while other times I was afraid that this might be hindering how far she had come. Although we appreciated everything that people were doing for us, I could not help but to be overprotective of Jenny early on in this stage of recovery.

Sometimes, we went for short walks, which were not easy for Jenny but made her smile. Before the accident, taking a walk together was one of those things she had always wanted me to do, but I had never wanted to go. For me, relaxing did not involve going for a walk. I preferred sitting on my front porch swing with a glass of bourbon on the rocks. Although doing so was relaxing and I miss it sometimes, it took away from my time with my wife. That invisible clock above our heads that is counting down to zero kept running as I spent time "relaxing" by myself. I realize now that I have wasted precious hours of this countdown of life being alone with a drink in my hand. After going on a few walks with Jenny, I realized just how special these moments are, not just to her, but to both of us. Our walks became moments when we could both share what we were going through and became important moments in our recovery as well as moments that have rebuilt our marriage.

Weeks went on and we slowly became adjusted to our

new normal life. I had to do many things around the house that I was not used to doing, and the reality that I had to return to work was not going to make any of this easier. I worked during the day and came home at night to cook, clean, help Jenny feed the children, give baths, change diapers, put the kids to bed, and the list goes on and on. Sometimes I just wanted to cry because I felt like this was going to be all that I did for the rest of my life. I did not want this life and, consequently, slipped into some dark places in my mind.

I knew that this was not Jenny's fault and that I needed to keep pushing through it all. I had periods when I became quiet and did not want to talk to anyone. Sometimes I romanticized about having a drink to help calm my nerves, but then I would think about how far I had come and that everything I was doing was significant in recovery for both of us. I pushed through it knowing that I only had to make it to tomorrow. Just like with my sobriety, I had to make it through today. Tomorrow would get a little easier than today was. We would both get a little stronger tomorrow. I just had to make it through today!

Jenny was getting frustrated as well. She likes to help and do things around the house, and it was killing her not to be able to help. It was also killing her to watch me get overwhelmed and frustrated. One evening we were sitting out on the back porch. Ruby was playing in her playhouse, and Charlie was swinging in his swing. Jenny was sitting in her wheelchair in what looked to be a depressive state. When I asked her if everything was ok, my wife started to cry as she said, "I don't want to be a burden to you. I know that this is hard for you." I looked at her and said, "Stop that right now. You are alive. I know that this will not be easy for any of us. Please ask me for help; tell me what you need. Yes, I am going to get frustrated, but it is ok. This is exactly what I signed up for. 'For better or for worse,' remember? Do not be afraid to ask me for help."

As each day went by, life did get a little easier. We had come up with a routine, and it was working. Jenny's mom was still at the house during the day helping with the daily activities of the house and all of the doctor appointments that she still needed to attend. I came home and took care of the family. Jenny even got to the point where she could help feed Charlie from her wheelchair. Slowly she progressed from a wheelchair to a one-handed walker to no walker at all. Daily physical therapy focused on strength. Occupational therapists worked with her to figure out how to work around the house with one arm. Jenny saw her counselor for mental rehabilitation and help with her PTSD. Doctor visits seemed endless, and they still do for that matter. Walks in the evenings with me, her mom, or one of her running friends helped strength her.

Over time, we were starting to click in the house as a unit again. Jenny still could not help the way that she wanted, but we were starting to see a glimmer of hope and she was starting to feel some of her freedom and independence that was abruptly taken away from her return. Now, how did I get her to want to drive again…

Welcome home, my love… We've missed you!

Twelve

her new car

Saturday, April 13, 2019
2:37 PM

Since her return home, a few new toys have come Jenny's way, including a new car. Driving a car had become just like riding a bike--something we take for granted and something that we simply know how to do. Whenever we need to get somewhere, we simply load up and go. Well, that is true until something as traumatic as Jenny's accident happens. When Jenny got home from the hospital, we had to start discussing her driving again and thinking about purchasing a new vehicle. The idea of getting behind the wheel again was not fun for her. Car shopping is one of those things that is supposed to be a joyous occasion, but this time for Jenny was not joyous; in fact, it was quite the opposite and something she dreaded. To ease her anxiety, I offered to take care of it if she liked, passing all decisions by her before we purchased her next car. She agreed and the search began.

Once again, so many questions arose in my mind: How could Jenny drive with one arm? Will she even be able to drive with one arm? Will she be able to drive at all due to the trauma associated with the accident? Does she even want a new car? Will she ever be able to drive alone? These questions worried me, but this is exactly how my mind works. I decided that I needed to quit questioning and trust that everything would work out.

One day the kids were at Jenny's parents' house, and we decided to look at a few cars. It was a wet, cool Saturday morning, and we knew that there would be no salesmen around to bother us. We drove onto the lot of our local dealership and made our way to the row of vehicles that had RAV4's on it. Jenny's other car had been an older model RAV4, so we wanted to check out the new ones to see if it was something that she might like owning once again. She immediately fell in love with the new ones, and we decided that I would come up do the dirty job of haggling the price down to something that we were willing to work with.

The following Monday, I went back to the dealership

and told the salesman a little bit of Jenny's story. I expressed interest in another RAV4 because we felt that Jenny's 2006 model was part of the reason that she was still alive today. I showed the salesman a picture of her wrecked vehicle and said, "This car flipped and rolled a number of times after taking a major impact on the driver's side door from another vehicle. Three people in it lived that day, so we trust the quality and really want to get into another one of these. I know what these sell for, I've done my research and I am willing to pay this amount for it. Can we make it work?" He was amazed at the picture of her old car and told me that he needed to talk to his boss but was sure that they would be able to help us. We took the new model for a test drive.

The salesman pointed out impressive safety features on this 2019 RAV4: Lane trace assist, Road sign assist, Pre-collision system with pedestrian detection, Full-speed range radar cruise control, Traction control, Anti-lock brakes, Smart-stop technology...The list went on and on, but what sold me was when he said, "Front and side impact airbags." I immediately started to think that if Jenny had had side impact airbags, she may still have her left arm. The improvements made in the safety of vehicles in a relatively short time were amazing. He agreed when I asked him if I could drive it home to show it to my wife since she could not come to the dealership.

I drove up to the house in this new shiny grayish silver

workhorse of a small-sized SUV and asked Jenny if she would like to look at it and let me take her for a ride in it. I wanted her to be one hundred percent sold before we purchased any vehicle. I knew that this was a huge decision for her and wanted her to feel safe in whatever she wanted to drive from this point on. She got inside and immediately fell in love with this car. I drove her out onto the highway and around the neighborhood doing my best salesman impression. I rattled off all of the bells and whistles the salesman at the dealership had just told me as we drove this beauty.

When we pulled up to the house, Jenny looked over to me and said, "I want to drive it." This would be the first time that she attempted to sit behind the wheel of a car since her accident, much less drive one. I parked the car in our driveway and we switched places. I told Jenny to take it slow and to pull over at any time if she felt that it was too much for her, that we could change places and it would be totally fine. She slowly backed out of the driveway and started down toward the end of the road. Watching her use one hand to take the car out of park, put it into reverse, back up, stop and shift it back into drive was nerve racking for me. At any point in this adventure, she could have had flashbacks and absolutely melt down, but she did not. Jenny slowly made her way down to the end of our street. She started to cry as we got to the stop sign. I asked if everything was ok; she simply nodded and said, "I'm ok. I just don't want to be scared" and kept driving. We made a short loop through a few streets in the neighborhood and went back home.

When we got home, I told her that I was extremely proud of what she had just accomplished and that we would take her driving in steps until she felt comfortable enough to drive on her own again. We had unlimited time to get her back on the road. I was not going to let her feel like she had to drive again anytime soon. After her traumatic experience behind the wheel, feeling comfortable driving again needed to be on her time, not anyone else's. Jenny loved the car and asked me to see if we could buy it. I got back to the dealership and told the salesman that we wanted it if he could get it into the price range I was offering. He agreed to my terms.

After signing an endless number of papers for the next few hours, I drove home in Jenny's new car. It was an exciting day for both of us because it represented one more step to recovery. Had Jenny told me that she never wanted to drive again, I would have respected that, but she did not. My wife was not going to let this trauma steal any more of her life. In fact, for the next few weeks, we went for daily drives around the neighborhood together. Each time we got into the car, she went a little farther than the last time. She was getting herself more familiar with the car and more comfortable with driving with the use of one arm.

One day Jenny told me that she wanted to take the

long loop through the neighborhood and back to our house. This meant facing a mile and a half stretch of the main highway, crossing oncoming traffic, and testing her mentally. I said, "Ok, if you think that you are ready, let's roll!" She took on this task with no problem, no tears, and seemingly zero anxiety. I am sure that there was a little anxiety inside her, but she did not show it. One thing that I can say without doubt about my wife is that she is a fighter; there is no denying that. I have said that since I met her, and she continues to prove that to me every day of her life. Now more than ever, she never ceases to amaze me with her willpower to overcome the adversity that has been set before her.

In late April, we decided to head out to Jenny's parents for the first time since the accident. She wanted to show off her new car to her family. If you cannot tell by now, there would be a lot of "firsts" in the months to come. If I were to describe the day, I would use the exact statement that I used in the opening of this book: "It was a cold, wet, damp humid Saturday morning…" The four of us loaded into the car and drove to the end of our street when Jenny asked if we could turn left and go the back way to her parents' house: She wanted to see where the accident happened. I asked if she was sure that she was ready to do that, and she said yes.

We turned left and silently headed that direction, retracing every mile of that ill-fated day. I did not say much or even ask many questions; neither of us did.

We just drove. I am sure that her mind and heart were racing with every mile that we drove and every turn that we made. The closer we got to the scene of the accident, the more nervous I began to feel. Jenny was likely feeling the same thing, but she remained silent.

We approached the intersection of Highway 35 and Granby, and I pulled the car over. The grass had grown up quite a bit in the ditch where the two cars hit their final resting places, but I could still make out the marks on the road and on the ground where the accident occurred. By the time we arrived, the rain was coming down heavily, so I asked if she wanted to get out to see where it all happened. She declined but said that she just wanted to look at everything from the car. I told her that I would walk out to the point in the road where the impact took place and then in the direction that both cars traveled. I would first show her where the other driver's car landed and then where her car landed. You see, what Jenny did not know is that I had come back to this site a few times while she was in the hospital to try to reconstruct in my mind what had taken place. It had become a place for me to think, to cry, and to ask for forgiveness for not being there with my family that morning. I had trouble letting go of the fact that I was not there and have had to deal with that in my own way. First, I dealt with it with a bottle of bourbon. Then, I dealt with it in rehab discussing it with my counselor. Finally, I dealt with it with talks between me and the Big Man upstairs. Sometimes I still have trouble letting the guilt go, but it gets easier as time passes.

I got out the car and walked to the middle of the north-bound lane where Jenny was traveling that day to show her where her life had officially changed. The marks on the road where the impact took place and where her skid marks started to turn to the right were still visible. I traced the steps to the location where both cars went off the road and down into the ditch. The bright orange paint was still visible, and the ground was still ripped up from the speed that these two vehicles entered into what I can only imagine were multiple flips and rolls. I then walked over to the tree line on the right side of the ditch where the other driver's car came to a stop. His car had faced back toward the highway. Then I walked down the ditch to the tree that looked like her car had hit before coming to its final resting spot also facing back toward the highway. I spent a few moments looking on the ground. Pieces of her car still lay on the ground, but what stuck out in my mind the most were the crayons.

A Ziploc bag of crayons lay on the ground next to the spot where Ruby and Charlie had been removed from the car. I looked back at the three of them sitting in Jenny's nice new car. All I could think of was how blessed I was to be standing in that moment, where time seemingly stopped, and they were all still alive. It could have been such a different ending. I could have been standing in that spot alone with a bottle of bour-bon in my hand asking for someone to take me out of my misery, but I was not. God saved them that day, and He saved me. I thanked Him as I made my way back to the car.

As I walked up the side of the ditch, a Jefferson Davis County Police officer stopped and politely asked what I was doing walking around in the ditch on a rainy day. I told him that I was there to look at the scene of the accident involving my wife and kids that had taken place a few months back. I added that my wife and kids were in the car and that she wanted to see where it had all happened. He said, "I worked that accident. You said she is in the car?" I replied, "Yes sir. This is the first time she has been back." He said, "Sir, take as much time as you need. I'm so glad that she is still here. None of us working the accident that night expected her to live." He walked back to his car and drove away.

I took a deep breath, looked back where it all happened one last time, and got back into the car. We have not returned to the scene since that day, and I do not know if we ever will. I left many emotions there that day. I realized that if I did not let go of the fact that I was not there for my family that day, I would never be able to move on with my own healing. I reached over and grabbed Jenny's hand. She did not smile, and she did not show any emotion. Instead, she simply shook her head and said, "Let's go." That is exactly what we did.

The next few months of driving were fun. It was as though I was riding with a teenager learning how to drive, but a very cautious one. Jenny drove up the road and back and then to the store and back. Any time we got into the car to go somewhere, she wanted to drive and I was good with that. To me, the more comfortable she got driving, the sooner she would get back to feeling normal and whole again. It was therapeutic for all of us, and she had been getting quite good at maneuvering her new car with one hand. Jenny began asking her mom and me if it was time for her to drive alone. We both looked at each other and said that we did not think that we were quite ready for her doing so just yet. We both wanted to keep her in the protective little bubble that she had been in since February for a little longer. Jenny laughed at us but did not push the issue.

The day for Jenny to drive alone finally came. Like a father not wanting his little girl to go out on her first date, I reluctantly agreed. Her maiden voyage would not be alone, and she was to report to me when she arrived at the Disneyworld of Hattiesburg--Target! She loaded into the car with Ruby in tow, and they both buckled up. I told her to be careful, and away they drove with smiles on their faces. They were like two teenagers rebelling and escaping the grips of their overprotective parents. They made it to Target and back without incident. Jenny came home drained physically and mentally, but it was another win for her, the beginning of the next big phase of her recovery.

Being able to drive without another adult in the car was beyond big. It was colossal in my book. Jenny had already proved to me that she was a superhero. At this point, I referred to her as Superwoman because that is exactly what she had become.

Thirteen

bionic woman

Wednesday, July 31, 2019
1:37 P.M.

Becoming comfortable with driving again enhanced Jenny's daily life. In addition to adjusting to operating her vehicle, another completely foreign task to master was operating a prosthetic arm and hand. Of course, with this came more questions: How do these prosthetics work? How will Jenny adapt to hers? Will we be able to afford what she needs? Does insurance cover the cost? These questions were soon be answered.

On Jenny's first night in the rehabilitation room, a tall man (tall to my standards, but I am only 5"7" on a good day) none of us had seen before approached us. Jenny and I probably had looks of wonder on our faces. He introduced himself to us as a representative from the Hanger Clinic, a prosthetic-making company here in Hattiesburg. Until this point, we had hardly even discussed the options for a prosthetic arm and had absolutely no clue what was available for upper extremity amputees. The only prosthetic arm I had ever remembered seeing was years ago on a man resembling Captain Hook. This gentleman's meeting with us was brief as he provided a very basic overview of what to expect when we went to the Hanger Clinic for Jenny's first visit in a few weeks. He asked if we had any questions, which we did not at the time, and went on his way.

His visit got us thinking about possibilities out there for Jenny. We had talked a little about it before now but were not knowledgeable about it. I suggested that Jenny research options during her free time and let me know what she wanted and that we would make it work, no matter the cost. I wanted her to be happy with whatever she wanted, and I wanted it to be the best product on the market if that is what she needed to help her feel normal again. The search began...

During my research of different types of prosthetics available for Jenny's arm, I learned that there are basically two types of upper extremity amputations-- the first being transhumeral, or above-the-elbow amputation, and the second being transradial, or below-the-elbow amputation. Jenny's amputation was transradial, which is the preferred option. She was left with approximately two inches below the elbow to work with when making her prosthetic. This did not mean much to me until our first meeting at the Hanger Clinic.

That first meeting took place about a week after Jenny's release from the hospital. We were to be joined by the gentleman who had visited us at the hospital and another man who comes into town on occasion specifically to work with upper extremity amputations. As we sat in the room waiting, I still had not researched the types of prosthetics available Jenny's transradial amputation. I am not sure why I had not done my research; maybe I pictured Jenny not wanting one. I pictured her running around after Charlie and snatching him up with one arm. I figured that she would adapt just fine with the use of one arm and that she would not even want a prosthesis. Or perhaps it was because somewhere deep down inside I did not want to face the fact that she had lost part of her body. I honestly do not know the answer to this day, but I do remember not thinking about it much. I just knew that everything was going to work out, no matter what she decided.

The door opened, and the two gentleman walked in. The hospital visitor was dressed in scrubs and introduced the other gentleman, who was dressed professionally. His accent indicated that he was not from the South. He was professional, caring, polite and really took his time to get to know about Jenny, our family, and the type of amputation that she had. He asked her many questions, being careful not to broach any subject that might upset her and reassured her that it was ok to pause and cry if she needed, adding that he was in no hurry.

He explained to us that Jenny's amputation looked like a "good" amputation, the type that would give her multiple options when it came to choosing a prosthetic. Having that two inches below her elbow made the process from building her arm to using her arm much easier than an above-elbow amputation. He asked Jenny if she had any ideas of what type of prosthetics were available to her, and, to my surprise, she rattled off a number of different types. He looked at all of us and said, "This woman has done her homework. That's good." He shook his head yes and said that with her amputation and the muscle movement that she still has in her arm, she could pretty much pick any type of prosthetic hand she would like to have. The options were endless!

Jenny had already narrowed her choices to two different styles of "bionic" hands that she had been watching videos about. She asked if he could explain how these worked and if they were viable options for her. He assured us that they would absolutely be options for her and added that they would work well with her type of amputation. He went on to explain exactly how each works. To this day, I am amazed by the process that takes place in the human mind that in order to control these hands.

He told Jenny to hold up her amputated arm. He said, "I want you to imagine that your hand is still attached to your arm. Pretend that you are holding your hand straight out with your thumb pointing up. Now, try moving your hand left and right, back and forth." When she did so, we all saw movement take place in what was left of the muscles in her forearm. He continued, "You see all of that movement? That is caused by your brain controlling the muscles that move your hand. This is how you will control your new hand." I am still in amazement to this day as to how all of this works. The forearm that would be molded to her arm and built for Jenny would have two little electrodes controlling the movement of her hand simply by flexing her muscles left and right. This was mind-blowing to us!

We immediately went home and got on Youtube to watch multiple videos of the two different bionic hand options that Jenny had been thinking about. For the first time, I got excited and saw the potential and benefit for her having one of these devices. Jenny smiled as she watched these videos and saw exactly what could be accomplished. We compared the two hands hundreds of times and finally decided on the Bebionic hand, which looks like something straight out of a movie. The individual fingers move, it opens and closes, and it has multiple settings that could benefit Jenny and assist her in doing daily activities both at work and at home. The most state-of-the-art prosthetic hand on the market, it had a price tag that confirmed it. Although we were worried about the cost, we had heard that with the insurance we had, we should be able to have the prosthetic covered by insurance up to eighty percent. With donations that had come in from people around the world, we should be able to cover the remaining cost of Jenny's Bebionic hand.

The next few visits to the Hanger Clinic consisted of measuring, fitting, molding, adjusting, refitting, etc. I missed accompanying Jenny on some visits due to being back at work full time, but Jenny's mom was always there for her on the days that I could not go. However, I did get to go to a few of the more important meetings during which Jenny had the opportunity to try on other hands while we waited for hers to arrive. The adjusting of all of the electrodes and the building of her socket and forearm was incredible to watch. She got to select fabric that was eventually to become her forearm and decided on a beautiful vibrant-yet-elegant floral pattern that fit her personality perfectly. When the forearm came it, it was simply beautiful! Watching the process unfold was truly amazing, as was the joy that each visit brought to her face. Jenny's new forearm was finished and ready. Now we had to wait for her new hand to arrive.

Jenny got a call from the Hanger Clinic saying that her hand was there and that she could come in the next day to try it on, see if everything was working properly, make any last-minute adjustments, and take it home. I planned to work a half day so that we could meet about lunchtime to head to the clinic and then spend the rest of this important day with her. I went home to pick her up, and off we went to the Hanger Clinic. Excitement was in the air for the both of us! It was an absolutely beautiful, sunny day and the weather was amazing. We both talked non-stop about the hand throughout our drive to the clinic; the anticipation was like that of kids on Christmas Eve wondering what Santa would bring them. When we arrived, we were brought back to the now-familiar room where Jenny had been multiple times over the past few months and waited for them to bring in her new hand.

The door opened, and the gentleman with whom Jenny had been working during this experience walked in with a big smile on his face. He seemed just as excited as we were to see this marvel in action. After reviewing every detail of the hand, he told Jenny exactly what to expect once she attached it to her forearm and turned it on. He told her not to worry if it did not work perfectly at first because he could adjust the sensitivity on the electrodes as needed until they had it perfect.

Jenny attached the hand to her forearm and turned it on as we alll sat with wonder and excitement on our faces. As the hand started to move, opening and closing perfectly, the biggest smile came across Jenny's face. That was the best moment of this important day! She lit up with excitement, smiling and laughing while trying out the different grip patterns that this hand would do. We spent the next thirty minutes or so in the clinic in amazement as Jenny learned the new options that could be done with this hand. Of course, she thanked the man who had been working with her over the past few months before we left.

We had lunch and took advantage of what free time we had left before picking up the kids from school. I soaked up every minute of that afternoon with Jenny. Her smiling face was all that I wanted and needed to see. For a moment, it was like nothing had even happened to her. Sitting across the table from her at the restaurant, I watched her fumble around with her new hand, trying to hold a skewer of shrimp with it while she used her fork with her right hand to take them off. It was absolutely beautiful to watch her and look into her eyes knowing that she was healing, both physically and emotionally. This gave her a sense of completeness, a knowing that she could do anything she wanted to do again. She may have lost part of her body, but this new apparatus opened the door to so many options that she had been worried about never being able to do again with only one hand. Once again, Jenny had regained a little more confidence and freedom.

Fourteen

love wins

Monday, August 5, 2019
8:57 P.M.

It's August 6, 2019, at 6:25 A.M. I help load Charlie and Ruby into the car as we all prepare to go to school and work. I go through my ritual, giving Ruby a kiss and saying, "I love you, Belle. Have a good day!" She replies, "I love you, too, Beast." I walk around and open Charlie's door, give him a kiss, and say, "I love you, Big Man!" Then I make my way to Jenny's window. I kiss her, look into her eyes, and say, "I love you."

She knows this is a tough moment for me, just as I know that it is equally difficult for her; we can see it in each other's eyes. She replies, "I love you, too!" She slowly and cautiously backs out the driveway. I watch as she puts the car in drive and pulls to the end of the street. Her left turn signal comes on, and my family pulls out of sight. This is the first time that they are all in the car again without me again since February 16, 2019. Standing there in a moment of solitude, I look up and say, "Thank you."

There have been times over the past months that I have wanted to give up on everything and run off to a secluded island by myself where nobody could find me. I could grow my hair long again, live in a camper, and invest my money in a bourbon distillery. I could be free as a bird without a care in the world, but I would still be haunted by the ghosts that hide deep down within. The reality of it all is that those ghosts have brought me moments of pain, anguish, self loathing, anxiety, and desperation, along with times when I cried out to God to end it all for me because I was too afraid to do it myself. These moments came and went, sometimes lasting a few days and sometimes lasting weeks on end. I hid them from the outside world. I hid behind the masks that we have all crouched behind from time to time. I prayed to God endlessly for something or someone to show me a way to salvation and to free me from the chains of guilt, humility, and shame that have been holding me down for so long.

One night I got that answer. I did not know it at the time, but what I did know was that I was about to embark on something totally unfamiliar to me. Earlier that same day, I had run into my friend at the grocery store. At home that evening, all I could do was think about the possibilities of writing this book and the different directions that I could take with it. When I went to bed that night, it was still on my mind. I had always been skeptical when it came to believing that someone could verbally hear the voice of God, but that night in my dream, a voice clearly said to me, "You must do this. You must get this out." I immediately woke up, sat up in bed, and thought to myself, "Do what?"

The next thing that came into my mind was to start writing this book. I looked at the clock and it was 2:37 A.M. I got out of bed, turned on my computer, and started typing whatever came to my mind. Here I am now, only three weeks later, writing chapter fourteen. I have not read a single word of what I have written since I wrote it. I am going to leave that up to my editor.

I have since made a vow to myself and to God that I am going to do whatever I can to try to forgive myself and move on from the foolish mistakes I have made in the past. Forgiving myself is not always easy. Even as I write this chapter, I cannot help but think of some of the things I have done that hurt my wife in our seventeen years together and cannot help but feel a little responsible for the accident, but I have forgiven myself. I grow stronger each day knowing that I have made an effort to be better than the person I was yesterday.

What drives me to keep going sometimes are two simple thoughts: When Jenny could have given up on life, she did not, and when Jenny could have and should have given up on me, she did not. I will never fully understand why she never left me, but I do not have to. I recently told her that I cannot forgive myself for the mistakes I made and the hurtful things I did while in my addiction. She looked at me and said, "I have forgiven you. No matter what it was, I have already forgiven you. Now it is time for you to forgive yourself."

Actor Matthew McConaughey once said something in an acceptance speech that I have never forgotten. His words sat dormant inside me for years until I woke up from the brain fog of depression and alcoholism. In his speech, he said,

"When I was 15 years old, I had a very important person in my life come and ask me, 'Who's your hero?' I said, 'I thought about it, and it's me in ten years.' So I turned 25 ten years later, and that same person came to me and said, 'Are you a hero?' I said, 'Not even close!' She said, 'Why?' and I said, 'My hero is me at 35.' You see, every day, and every week, and every month, and every year of my life, my hero is always ten years away. I'm never going to be my hero. I'm not going to obtain that, and that's fine with me because it keeps me with somebody to keep chasing. So to any of us, whatever those things are and whatever it is we

look up to, whatever it is we look forward to and who-ever it is we're chasing, to that I say, 'Amen.'"

Until recently I did not follow philosophy, but now I chase that person every day. I know that I will never catch him, but I know that if I keep trying, I can only become a better person to everyone around me.

Both Jenny and I still have times where we struggle with getting through the day. Doing daily chores, homework, kids, being a husband and a wife. Do we still get overwhelmed, angry, and frustrated? We do indeed, and we have every right to feel that way. What keeps us going is our love for each other and the grace we have gained through the many trials we have faced. This is the real us. This is our life. This is what makes us who we are. Yes, we both still see counse-lors when we need people to talk to, but for me, writing this book has been a saving grace--a way to let it all go, a way for me to express openly the way I feel, and a way for me to stay accountable in my sobriety.

Life is definitely not always easy for any of us. For all the beautiful posts you see on social media, there are a thousand bad moments in between that are never discussed in public. However, those are the moments that build our family, the moments that make us stronger, and the moments that nobody can ever take away from us. Without trying moments, life would be easy. However, life is not easy, and you have to fight for what you really want. We have fought the good fight and we have won. When this journey started, Jenny literally fought to stay alive, and I fought not to drink myself to death. We both fought to stay alive through rehabilitation of our own. Although our rehabilitations required different paths, in some ways they are similar. We have rehabilitated our bodies, minds, and souls. In a way, we have both been at our rock bottoms, and have come out sober in so many different ways. In time, we know that some of these moments and memories will fade and life will get easier. It already has, but we also hold on to some of the pain is associated with all of this.

Holding on to these events will always be a reminder for me of where I am today and where I do not want to return. We do much more as a family now. Our walks in the evenings have become therapy sessions for the entire family. They have become our time to disengage from the rat race around us and to check in and reconnect with each other. I cannot speak for Jenny here, but I formerly tried to fight my inner battles alone or cover them up with alcohol. It seemingly was the easy way out, but now we walk through this life together. We talk through things that are bothering us. We know that we are stronger as a team. Perhaps most importantly, we know that in the end, love wins.

Our story does not end here; in fact, it is simply the beginning--the beginning of a new life for both of Jenny and me, a rebirth from our past mistakes and a reset on life. When a trauma like this takes place, life does not have to end. You can either drown yourself in misery, sorrow, and a bottle of liquor until you emotionally and physically die, or you can choose to look up and live. If you ever find yourself in a situation like this, what choice will you make? Our choice is to write another chapter, to educate others about life after trauma and life after sobriety, and to finish our story, together.

Jenny Maul updated her status
October 4
Love wins @chrismaulphotography

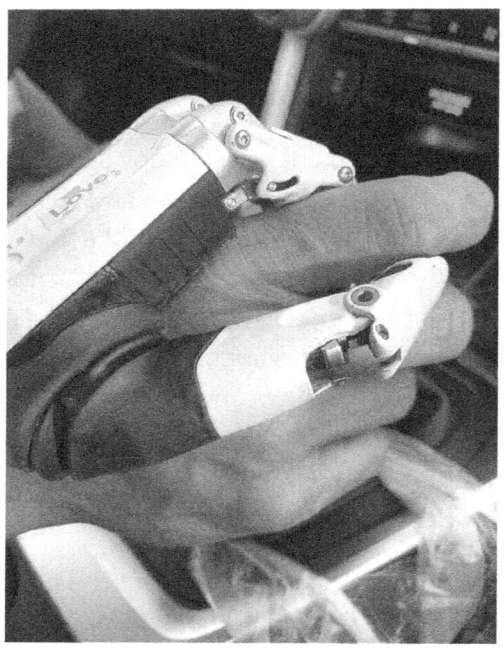

Psalm 30
A David Psalm

I give you all the credit, God—
 you got me out of that mess,
 you didn't let my foes gloat.
²⁻³ God, my God, I yelled for help
 and you put me together.
God, you pulled me out of the grave,
 gave me another chance at life
 when I was down-and-out.

Luke 1:15

"For he shall be great in the sight of the Lord, and
shall drink neither wine nor strong drink; and he shall
be filled with the Holy Ghost, even from his mother's
womb."

The Serenity Prayer

God, grant me the serenity to accept the things I
cannot change,
Courage to change the things I can,
And wisdom to know the difference.

Thank You

I would be remiss if I did not express special words of gratitude to our parents. Jenny and I are truly blessed to be their children.

To my mom, Pamela Maul, I love you with all my heart. You have been an outlet for me over the past few months to share my ups and downs. Thank you for not judging me too harshly when I needed to share some of my past experiences with you. I knew that you would understand exactly what I was going through during my recovery process and during the process of being a caregiver. You have experienced both situations, and I cannot thank you enough for being that listening ear.

To my dad, Robert Maul, I admire you daily. I applaud your strength and perseverance even more now that I know what you have gone through during forty years of sobriety. We have had some amazing conversations during my recovery--conversations that speak volumes. There are no words that I can put on paper to thank you enough for what you have personally done for me in this lifetime. I love you.

My mom and dad have been nothing but supportive throughout all of this experience. Although I was not able to communicate much with them in the beginning because I did not have much time to reach out initially, they have been there for me. I have always had supportive parents, but over the past year, I have been able to count on them more than ever, even if just for a familiar, reassuring voice. You two have made me the person that I am today.

To Jenny's mom, Becky Wigington, the support and unconditional love that you have shown our family have been inimitable, and the faith that you exhibit daily is beautiful. You and I have been through some good and bad times together, some worth sharing and others that will remain between just the two of us. We went from trying to figure out what to do each day to becoming a well-oiled machine that made everything work out. I could not have done this without you. Thank you for your unending love and support, especially throughout this past year. It will never be forgotten.

To Jenny's dad, David Wigington, who is not mentioned much in this book because he had to keep on with the daily flow of his and Jenny's mom's life in the outside world, I have learned so much from watching your actions.

After the accident, you took watch over Jenny many nights in the hospital, getting no sleep and then going to work the next day without complaining. I witnessed you on your knees in the hospital crying out to God to help Jenny. You are a true example to me and to many of what a God-fearing husband and father should be to his children.

Jenny's dad could have turned his back on me when he found out about my alcoholism, but he did not. He came to me one day, looked me in the eyes, and said,

"If you ever need to talk, I'm here and I love you." Honestly, I am not sure if he was talking about Jenny's wreck or if this was his way of telling me that he knew what was going on with me and that it was going to be fine, but the look in his eyes was unmistakable. It was not the look of a man who once did not approve of me. (My father-in-law and I did not always see eye-to-eye when Jenny and I first met. Now that I have a daughter, I cannot blame him for wanting to do anything he could to protect his daughter; in fact, I feel the same way.) Instead, it was the look of a man who knew that I was in pain, a man who was sharing my pain and knew that I needed his approval. This single moment let me know that I could handle everything being thrown my way and that I did not have to do it alone. Thank you for that support.

To all of our other family members who are not specifically mentioned, know that we could not have done this without each of you. Thankfully, the Maul and Wigington families are strong. Without this deeply rooted family system, this branch of the family tree could have broken and died out. Instead, I see a beautiful tree that will continue branching out in both faith and love.

I also want to thank many people who are never named in this book. We appreciate every person who has helped us and could not have gotten this far without your donations, prayers, positive vibes, support, and, most importantly, your love. Thank you for everything you have done for us; we will never be able to repay you. We are blessed that you are a part of our lives.

When I first started writing this, I attempted to include everyone who supported us in this journey but quickly decided that including that many names would take away from what I was trying to convey. With the exception of eyewitness reports, I used only the names of my family--Chris, Jenny, Ruby and Charlie, the four people who survived this nightmare and have awakened on the other side of it as a stronger team.

This book is just the beginning of our new story of victory and our celebration of life. Jenny and I look forward to growing old together, watching our beautiful children grow into adults, and writing this great novel called life.

About the Author

Chris is a respected educator and photographer in his hometown of Hattiesburg, MS. He is a native of Lakeland, FL where he grew up as the youngest of three brothers. Chris attended the University of Southern Mississippi where he met his wife, Jenny in Hattiesburg. There, they put down roots and started a family. Through the years he developed a great love for writing. Until now, his writings have been private. But after a traumatic life altering event, he felt compelled to share his journey of trauma and alcoholism publicly. Writing became an essential part of Chris's healing.

If you or anyone else has a problem with substance abuse, please do not stay silent. You do not have to do this alone. Chris has dedicated his live to helping others with the disease of addiction. Reach out to him if you ever need someone to talk to. You will never be judged; you will only find a place of love and acceptance with Chis.

~ Jenny Maul

Made in the USA
Columbia, SC
19 March 2020